COLLINS GEM

CHESS

David Longrigg and
The Diagram Group

D1517624

HarperCollins*Publishers*

HarperCollins Publishers
P.O. Box, Glasgow G4 0NB

A Diagram book first created by Diagram Visual
Information Limited of 195 Kentish Town Road,
London NW5 8SY

First published 1994

Reprint 10 9 8 7 6 5 4 3 2 1 0

© Diagram Visual Information Limited 1994

ISBN 0 00 470641 2

Printed in Great Britain by
HarperCollins Manufacturing, Glasgow

Introduction

The origins of the game of chess are obscure, and it is not until the 7th century that there is a reference to chess in literature. Evidence suggests that chess first took root in India, and spread to Europe by way of the Moors invading Spain in the 8th century. The Muslims also conquered Sicily, and the game reached Russia probably through the Caspian–Volga trade routes. The Vikings carried the game to north-western Europe via the Baltic, and gradually the game spread throughout all the countries of Europe. Today there are 149 countries belonging to FIDE – Fedération Internationale des Échecs – founded in 1924.

Why did this game spread and become international in the last 200 years? Simply because it's exciting, it demands skill, and the result is unpredictable. It's a war game. But it's not a physical contest, and there is no element of luck as in card games. In oriental warfare, a battle could be decided by the death or capture of the king, which in chess is known as Shah–mat (checkmate).

So two armies line up against each other. One can try head-on assault or patient outflanking manoeuvres. One can try bluff, or offer poisoned pawns, or make sacrifices in order to ambush the enemy and capture the commander-in-chief, the king.

How do the pieces move? What are the traps? How can I outflank the enemy and get round the back? Can the king be attacked, or the queen captured? Is my king safe from assault? What shall I do with the infantry –

the pawns? The knight is the only piece on a horse, so it is the only piece that can jump; but where should it jump to?

I hope that by concentrating on this elementary introduction to chess, the reader will gain enough knowledge to be a confident player and will have a wide enough basis to search more deeply into chess literature. But the best practice is to play the game.

David Longrigg, 1994

Contents

1. Preparation

THE PIECES
Chess pieces – a Staunton pattern

Each player starts with 16 pieces; 1 king, 1 queen, 2 rooks, 2 bishops, 2 knights and 8 pawns.

Piece	Notation	Symbol	Staunton set pieces
King (a)	K		
Queen (b)	Q		a b
Rook (c) (sometimes called castle)	R		
Bishop (d)	B		c d
Knight (e)	N		
Pawn (f)	P		e f

THE BOARD

1 The board must be 64 squares

2 When a chess diagram is printed:

- Black is at the top – playing down.
- White is at the bottom – playing up.

3 The top left and bottom right squares must be white

4 There is a wide variety of chess sets, but it is advisable to play with a Staunton-pattern chess set. These are used in school games and club matches. Howard Staunton, actor and Shakespearean scholar, was the best player in the world in 1843.

Black

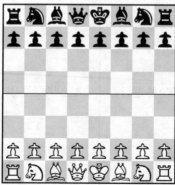

White

The sides of the board

Queenside

The 32 squares to the left of the board – looking at the board as if you are playing from the white side.

Kingside

The 32 squares to the right of the board – looking at the board as if you are playing from the white side.

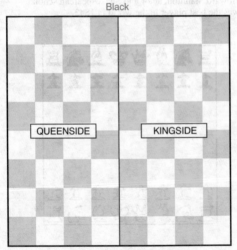

Black

QUEENSIDE   KINGSIDE

White

The squares on the board
Each of the 64 squares on the board has a letter and a number which refer to a rank and a file.

Ranks
Ranks are the full horizontal lines across the board represented by the numbers 1–8 from bottom to top.

Files
Files are the vertical lines up and down the board represented by letters a–h from left to right.

Black

a8	b8	c8	d8	e8	f8	g8	h8
a7	b7	c7	d7	e7	f7	g7	h7
a6	b6	c6	d6	e6	f6	g6	h6
a5	b5	c5	d5	e5	f5	g5	h5
a4	b4	c4	d4	e4	f4	g4	h4
a3	b3	c3	d3	e3	f3	g3	h3
a2	b2	c2	d2	e2	f2	g2	h2
a1	b1	c1	d1	e1	f1	g1	h1

White

NOTATION

Writing a move

- A capital letter indicates the piece which is moving, (except for the pawn, see p.22).
- After the letter of the piece comes the small letter of the file and then the number of the rank.
- Check (see p.52) is +.
- A capture (see p.27) is x.
- Castling on the kingside (see p.33) is 0-0 and castling on the queenside (see p.34) is 0-0-0.
- Checkmate is normally written as mate.
- When a pawn reaches the 8th rank, it is 'promoted' to a new piece of the player's choice. Examples are: g8/Q and d1/N (see p.24).

Example A – Some possible moves in Diagram A

White moves:

- Bb5+   (bishop to b5 square and check).
- Qa4+   (queen to a4 square and check).
- Bxb4   (bishop captures, or takes, bishop).
- a3   (pawn on a-file moves to a3 square).

Black moves:

- ...Nc6   (knight to c6 square).
- ...Bd7   (bishop to d7 square).
- ...0-0   (castling on the kingside).
- ...Qe7   (queen to e7 square).
- ...Bxd2+   (bishop captures, or takes, bishop and check).

Two pieces to the same square

If there is a possibility of two similar pieces moving to the same square or rank (Diagram B), then the small letter after the capital letter of the piece indicates the file the piece is on before it moves.

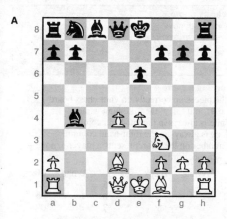

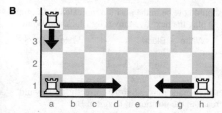

The notation of the above moves is Rad1, Rhf1 and R4a3.

> **Other symbols**
>
> | ! | = Good move | ? | = Poor move |
> |---|---|---|---|
> | !! | = Very good move | ?? | = Very bad move; |
> | ?! | = Dubious | | a blunder |
> | !? | = Interesting | | |

Recording a game

Set the pieces up correctly on your chess board
(see p.9), and 'play' the following game.

● White is always in the left-hand column.
● Black is always in the right-hand column.

The number on the left represents a player's move –
first, second, third, etc.

	White	Black			White	Black
1	e4	e5		5	0-0	Be7
2	Nf3	Nc6		6	Re1	b5
3	Bb5	a6		7	Bb3	0-0
4	Ba4	Nf6				

You should now be in the position indicated in Diagram
A. Now play the next five moves by Black and White.

	White	Black			White	Black
8	c3	h6		11	d4	exd4
9	Bc2	d6		12	cxd4	d5
10	h3	Bb7				

If you have made moves 8 to 12 correctly, you should
have reached the position in Diagram B.

(Don't worry about the game itself – just concentrate
on the recording to begin with).

A

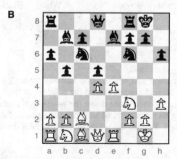

B

Descriptive notation

This type of notation is now out of fashion, but it was used in nearly all chess books and articles some years ago, so it is useful to know how to follow a game written in descriptive notation.

Each square has two identifications, one from Black's point of view, and the other from White's. In descriptive notation the a- and h-files are R-files; the b- and g-files are N-files; the c- and f-files are B-files; the d-file is the Q-file; and the e-file the K-file. The ranks are numbered 1–8 for the White moves, but 8–1 for the Black moves. If there is any ambiguity about a move, then the file letter is preceded by K for kingside or Q for queenside (see White's second move in the following sequence). So the first seven moves of the game given on page 14, leading to Diagram A, would be recorded as follows:

	White	Black		White	Black
1	P-K4	P-K4	5	0-0	B-K2
2	N-KB3	N-QB3	6	R-K1	P-QN4
3	B-N5	P-QR3	7	B-N3	0-0
4	B-R4	N-B3			

Recording a position

If for any reason you wish to stop halfway through a game, you should always record the position of the pieces on the board. Write down the position of each piece using its letter symbol and then the square of the board it is on. Record the white pieces and then the black.

The position in Diagram B would be recorded as follows:

Ke3 Rb2 Pa3 Pd4 Pf4 Pg3 Ph2 v Kf7 Rc4 Pa6 Pb5 Pf6 Pg7 Ph7

A

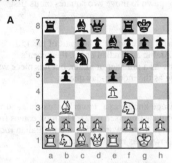

B

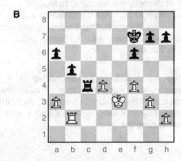

THE HISTORY OF PIECES

The laws of chess and the movement of the pieces have been the same since the 16th century. The changes that took place have quickened up the rate of play, such as allowing the pawn to move two squares on its first move.

Queen

Not a powerful piece until the last part of the 15th century. In Arabic and Indian chess, the queen's predecessor was a minister or vizier, but this piece was not as strong as the modern-day queen.

Rook

Often in Europe known as a 'tower' or 'castle', and we still talk about castling (see p.32). The rook comes from the Persian and Arabic word *rukh*, and the Italian *rocco*. The rook's power has remained unchanged.

Bishop

The history of the bishop is not clear. In medieval England the power of the Church was recognized in naming the piece a bishop. But the English bishop is an elephant in Russia, a messenger in Germany, and a court jester in France.

Knight

In Chaturanga, which is the earliest known type of chess, the knights were war-horses. In many countries knights were part of the cavalry. In Germany, the word *springer* means leaper or jumper. The knight's power has remained unchanged.

Pawns

The Arabs called them *baidaq*, foot soldiers, which was translated into the Anglo-French word *p'oun*. In the old game, a pawn could not be promoted to a queen, but to a minister only. The strategy of chess was, therefore, different from today, for there was little point in promotion (see p.24).

King

The king in the 13th century was allowed to make a leap, but only once in a game, and from this came the idea of castling (see p.32). Otherwise, the king's movement has always been the same.

MOVEMENT OF THE PIECES

The king
1 The king can move one square, in any direction.

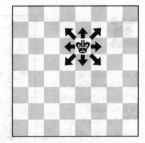

The queen
1 The queen can
move any number
of squares –
diagonally, vertically
or horizontally.
2 The queen cannot
'jump' over another
piece on the same line.

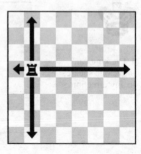

3 The queen is the most powerful of all the pieces.

The rook
1 The rook can
move any number
of squares, vertically
or horizontally.
2 The rook cannot
'jump' over another
piece.

The bishop
1 The bishop can move any number of squares diagonally.
2 The bishop cannot 'jump' over another piece.

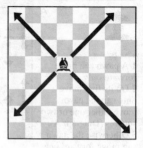

The knight
1 The knight moves two squares in one direction horizontally or vertically, and then one at right angles.
2 The knight *can* 'jump' over other pieces.

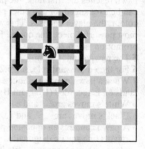

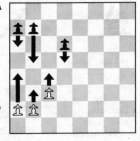

The pawn

1 A pawn can move forward only.

2 On its first move only can the pawn move either one or two squares (Diagram A).

3 Otherwise the pawn can move forward one square only (Diagram A).

4 If a white pawn reaches the eighth rank, or a black pawn reaches the first rank, the pawn is 'promoted' and can be exchanged for any other piece, of the same colour, the player chooses. This will usually be the most powerful piece, the queen. For the rules of promotion, see p.24.

5 The pawn cannot 'jump'.

6 For the **en passant** rule, see p.24.

7 When a pawn moves without a capture, the square it lands on is recorded (Diagram B).

● White's moves are a3 and c4.

● Black's moves are ...b5 and ...d6.

8 A pawn captures an opposing piece by moving forwards one square diagonally. When a pawn makes a capture a player records the file it started on and the square it lands on (Diagram C).

● White's capture is fxe3.

● Black's capture is ...gxf6.

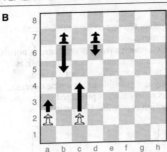

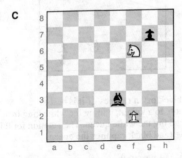

Promotion

- A pawn is promoted on reaching the last rank as part of the same move.
- The square on which a pawn is promoted is normally called the queening square, even if the pawn is exchanged for a piece which is not a queen.
- Theoretically it is possible to have nine queens.
- The pawn is nearly always promoted to a queen, but underpromotion is possible (Diagram A).

A

When the black pawn reaches g1 it is best to underpromote to a knight, putting the white king in check and taking the white queen. The notation for this is 1...g1/N+ (and black captures the queen).

En passant (In passing)

1 The en passant capture can only be made by a pawn on its 5th rank.

2 If an enemy pawn on an adjoining file is moved two squares in one move, it can be captured.

3 This must be done immediately or not at all.

4 The en passant move is optional, not obligatory.

5 Beginners often find this difficult, so practice on the 5th and 7th ranks of both Black and White.

The en passant move

In Diagram B Black to move.

In Diagram C Black moves 1...c5.

B

C

In Diagram D White moves 2 bxc6 (en passant). Note the move is 2 bxc6 en passant not 2 bxc5 en passant. Imagine the black pawn has only moved one square.

D

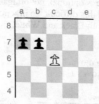

Diagram E shows some further en passant moves.

White to move
1 a4 bxa3 e.p.
1 c4 bxc3 e.p.
1 c4 dxc3 e.p.

Black to move
1...h5 2 gxh6 e.p.
1...f5 2 gxf6 e.p.
1...f5 2 exf6 e.p.

E

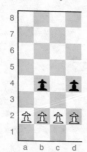

CAPTURING

- To capture a piece means to deprive your opponent of the use of that piece. It has been taken and leaves the board.
- All pieces, except the pawn (see p.31), capture by moving to a square they can normally move to (Article 4.3) and capturing the opponent's piece situated there.

Capturing with the king

The king can capture any piece that is on an adjacent square, providing the king is not moving into check.

A 1 Kxf1 or 1 Kxg2

Capturing on the diagonals

The queen and bishops can capture any piece on the
diagonals, providing there is not another piece in the
way. In Diagram B:

- Black has lost a rook. White's queen has won/taken a
  rook.
- White has lost a knight. The black bishop has won/
  taken a knight.

B 1 Qxa7 Bxh6

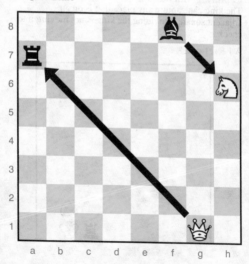

Capturing on the ranks and files

The queen and rook can capture on the ranks and files, providing there is nothing in the way. In Diagram C:

- Black has lost a pawn. White's queen has won/taken a pawn.
- White has lost a knight. The black rook has won/taken a knight.

C 1 Qxb7 Rxf8

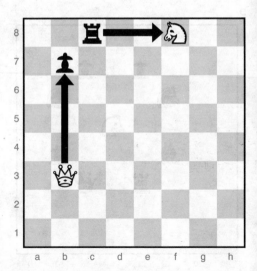

Capturing with the knight

The knight – the only piece that can jump – can take any
piece on a square that the knight can legally move to.

In Diagram D the white knight has eight possible
captures:

- 1 Nxf7
- 1 Nxg6
- 1 Nxg4
- 1 Nxf3
- 1 Nxd3
- 1 Nxc4
- 1 Nxc6
- 1 Nxd7

D

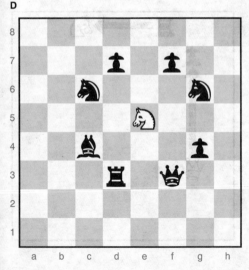

Capturing with the pawn
The pawn can only capture one diagonal square forward to its left or right.

Diagram E shows four white and black pawn captures:

- 1 bxa3
- 1 bxc3
- 1 fxe3
- 1 fxg3

- 1...bxa6
- 1...bxc6
- 1...gxf6
- 1...gxh6

E

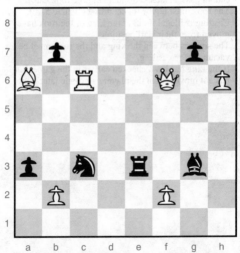

CASTLING

When a player castles, the king and rook move
simultaneously, as part of the same move. The king
always moves two squares to the left or right depending
on if the move is on the queenside or kingside. The
rook moves two squares in a kingside castling move
and three squares in a queenside castling move. The
following rules must also be followed:

- The king cannot castle out of check.
- The king cannot castle through check. (The king
  cannot pass an attacked square but the rook can.)
- The rook must not be touched first (Article 5.1c).
- Castling is illegal if either the king or the rook have
  moved from their start positions.
- The squares between the king and the rook must be
  vacant before castling.
- If the king has been checked earlier in the game, but
  has not moved, then the player can castle later.

Kingside castling
(notation symbol 0-0)

Before castling Black

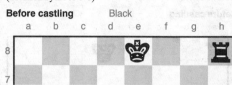

After castling

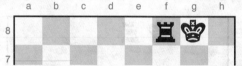

Before castling White

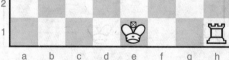

After castling

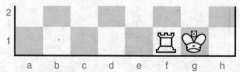

Queenside castling
(notation symbol 0-0-0)

Before castling   Black

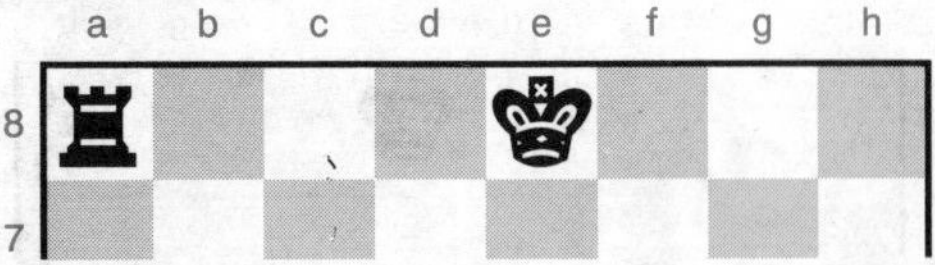

After castling

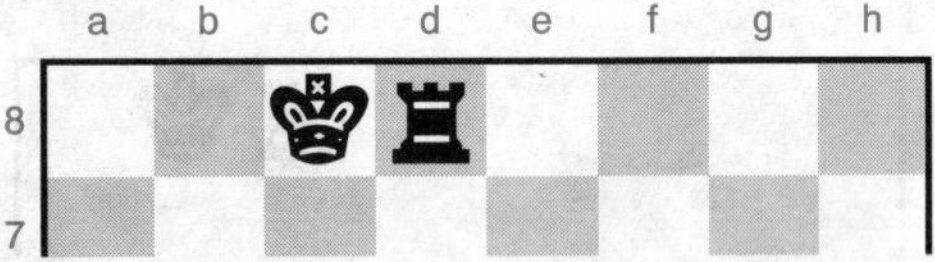

Before castling   White

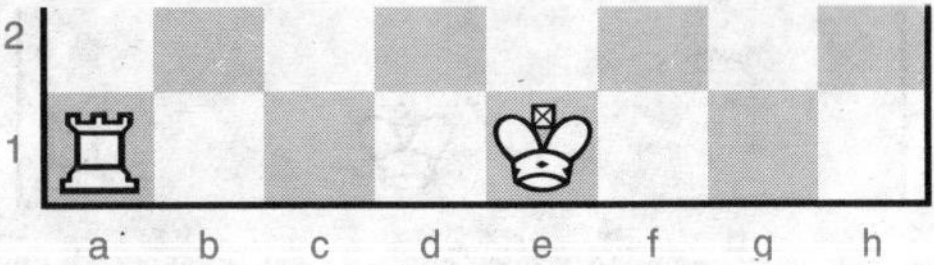

After castling

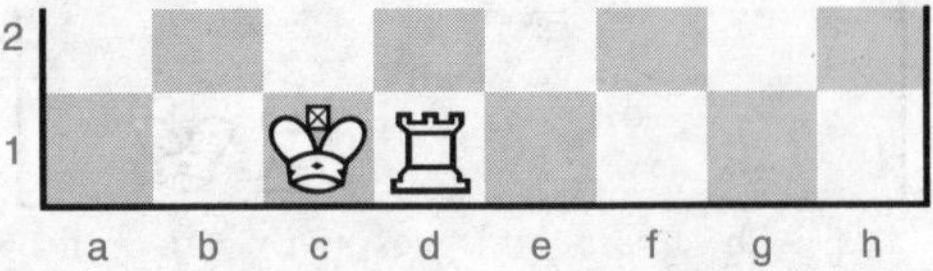

VALUES OF THE PIECES

Some pieces are, of course, more valuable than others. But often the value of a piece depends on its position on the board and what it can do in that position. Here is a rough guide to the value of pieces, with a pawn being worth one point.

Major pieces

Minor pieces

| Q = 9 | R = 5 | B = 3 | N = 3 |

The major pieces are queens and rooks and the minor pieces are bishops and knights. But a bishop, for instance, stuck behind its own pawns, or in a corner, is not as powerful as a central knight with more freedom of movement. In exchanging pieces, there should therefore be some evaluation. The following equations will help you in play when you are considering sacrifices and planning moves:

- N or B = three pawns
- B or N + two pawns = R
- B + N = R + one pawn
- B + N + N = Q
- R + R = Q + one pawn

A COMPLETED GAME

A game of chess is won when:

- A player checkmates the opponent's king (Article 10.1).
- A player resigns.
- A player loses on time.

A game of chess is drawn when:

- Stalemate occurs. This results when the player to move is not in check and is unable to make a legal move (see Diagrams A, B, C).
- Both players agree to a draw (Article 10.6).
- 'Upon a claim by the player having the move, when the same position, for the third time is about to appear or has just appeared, the same player having the move each time...' (Article 10.10).
- When fifty consecutive moves have been made by each side, with neither a piece being taken, nor a pawn being moved (Article 10.12).
- When only king v king remains.
- When king v king with only bishop or knight remains.
- When king and bishop v king and bishop remains, with both bishops on diagonals of the same colour.

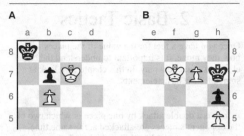

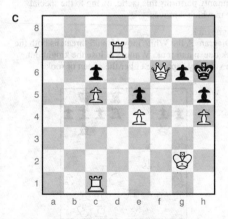

2. Basic Tactics

Once you have a feel for the value of the pieces and how they move, it is important to understand the basic elements of tactical play. In this chapter, we look at some of these basic elements.

FORKS

A fork is a double attack by one piece in which two of the opponent's pieces are attacked at the same time. Any piece can fork, though it is the knight that most commonly performs this tactic, owing to the special way in which it moves.

Knight fork

In Diagram A the White move 1 Nd5 threatens both the black queen and rook. White will lose the knight but gain value by capturing either the queen or rook.

A

In Diagram B White has not castled, so the white king is still in the centre of the board. The black knight on c2 checks the king, and forks king, queen and rook! Forking more than two pieces is called a family fork.

B

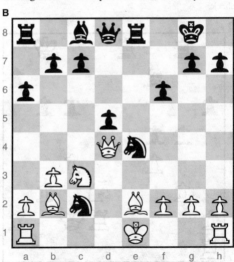

In Diagram C 1 Nd5 forks Black's bishop and f-pawn. Black is unable to counter both threats and thus loses a pawn. Black will either move or defend the bishop when White will capture the f-pawn, incidentally giving check.

C

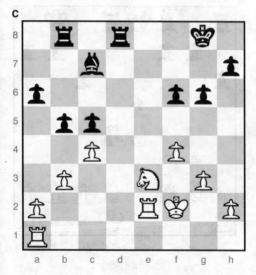

Queen fork

In Diagram D Black has castled and partially developed. But, White to move, Black is in danger. 1 Bxf6 Bxf6. What is White's next move which leads to the capture of the black rook on a8?

D

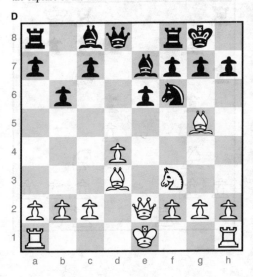

Answer: 2 Qe4 (if 2...Rb8, then 3 Qxh7 mate).

Rook fork

In Diagram E, if White moves 1 Rc7, Black is unable to defend both bishops and thus loses a piece.

E

Bishop fork

How does White capture a black rook?

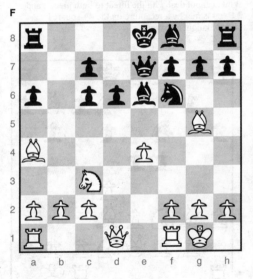

Answer: 1 Bxc6+

Pawn fork

In Diagram G Black to move plays 1...d4. This move
forks the white knight on c3 and the bishop on e3.
White cannot deal with the threat to both pieces, and
2 Bxd4 is met by a recapture on the d4-square by
bishop, knight or pawn.

G

PINS

A pin occurs when a lower value piece is unable to move due to the potential threat to a higher value piece situated behind it. This higher value piece is often the king.

● The pin is one of the most powerful tactical elements.
● A piece pinned is a paralysed piece.

In Diagram A the knight is pinned. It cannot move, as otherwise the king would be in check.

A

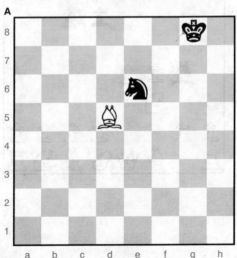

In Diagram B the black bishop pins the white knight.
To counter this the a2 pawn could move to a3, attacking
the bishop.

B

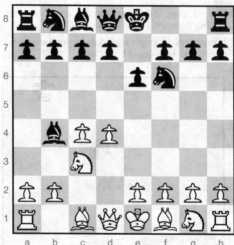

In Diagram C Black's knight and bishop are pinned. It is White to move. What material advantage can White achieve (see Diagram D)?

C

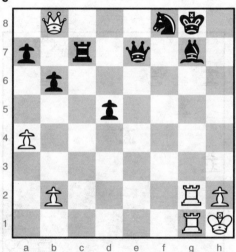

The following moves are played out from Diagram C.

	White	Black
1	Rxg7+	Qxg7
2	Qxc7	(Diagram D)

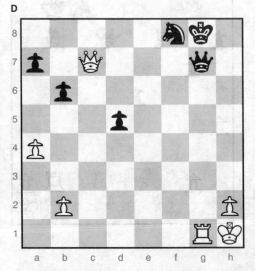

White has won a piece and has a rook against knight – a winning advantage. After 2...Ng6 White exchanges queens with an easy win.

SKEWERS

Similar to a pin, but not the same. A skewer is an attack along a file, rank or diagonal which threatens a high-value piece. After that piece has moved, another lower value piece is exposed.

In Diagram A the black queen must move to avoid capture. After the queen moves, White captures the black rook with the move 1 Bxh7.

A

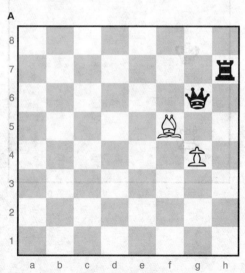

In Diagram B the black king is in check. It must move, but White then plays 1 Rxb8.

B

In Diagram C Black has just moved. With White to move, can you see the skewer which will eventually win the game for White?

C

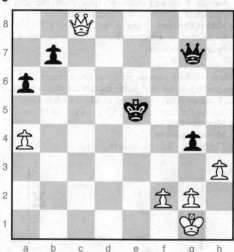

Answer: 1 Qc3+

CHECK AND CHECKMATE

- The whole point of the game is to capture or kill the king. Chess is a war game!
- If the king is in check, it is threatened and must escape capture. If the king cannot escape capture, then it is in checkmate, usually abbreviated to mate.
- *Shah* is Persian for ruler or king, and *mat* is Persian for helpless or defeated. Over the centuries *shah-mat* became checkmate.

Getting out of check

There are three ways to get out of check; move the king; interpose with another piece; capture the checking piece. In Diagram A the black rook checks the white king. What are the three ways the king can get out of check?

- Move the king to g1.
- Move the rook to h2.
- The bishop takes the rook (Bxh5).

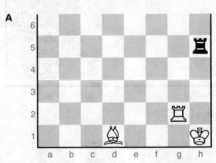

In Diagram B the white queen checks the king.

- The king cannot move to a7 because kings cannot stand next to each other.
- The only move out of check is 1...Bb8.

B

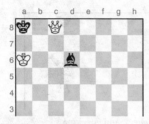

In Diagram C the white rook checks the king. What are the three ways to escape check?

- Move the king to b8, b7, d8 or d7.
- Interpose with the black bishop with 1...Bc7.
- Capture the attacking piece with 1...dxc5, the best move in this position.

C

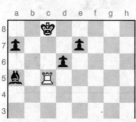

Discovered check
One piece moves so that another piece checks the king.
In Diagram D the move 1 Bg6+ leaves the king in
check by the white rook.

D

Examples of check and checkmate
In Diagram E the white queen checks the king.
How does Black capture the white queen?

E

Answer: 1...Rf2+

In the following checkmates (Diagrams F and G) none of the three escapes from check is available, so the king is checkmated.

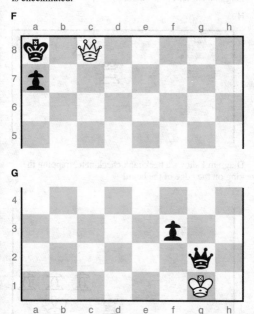

Rook checkmates

Diagram H shows a two rook checkmate, trapping the king in a corner of the board.

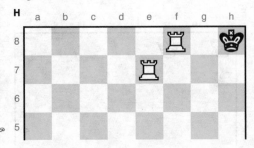

Diagram I shows a back rank checkmate, trapping the king on the edge of the board.

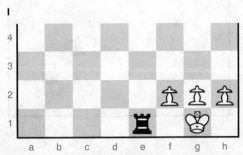

Bishop checkmates

The two bishops in Diagram J control the diagonals coming from a1 and b1. The black king on b3 stops the white king from moving to a2.

J

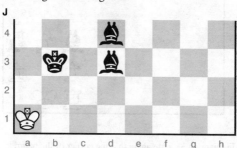

Note that you often need an extra piece to help two bishops get a checkmate (Diagram K).

K

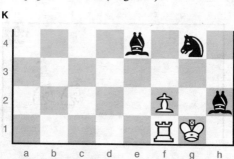

Knight checkmates
In Diagram L the white king has no escape.

L

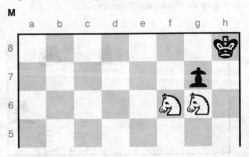

In Diagram M, note again that the corner of the board is important in obtaining checkmate.

M

Smothered mate

In Diagram N the king cannot move; it is 'smothered' by its own pieces. The knight is the only piece that can check through other pieces.

3. Further tactics

SACRIFICES AND COMBINATIONS

It is impossible to say when the opening finishes and the middlegame begins, for there is no clear demarcation point. Very roughly, the middlegame is that part of the game which follows development when most pieces are still on the board. Sacrifices and combinations make up a big part of the middlegame where you plan to defeat your opponent.

Having mastered the basic movement of the pieces, it is important to develop a feel for how the pieces combine together. The loss of a piece (which is usually caused by a tactical oversight) invariably implies the loss of the game. In this chapter we will examine various typical tactical themes and ideas which you should watch out for.

These are:
- Double attack.
- Discovered attack.
- Discovered check.
- Deflection.
- Decoying.
- Removing the defender.
- Blockading.

DOUBLE ATTACK

A double attack involves, as its name implies, the creation of two simultaneous threats. These may simply consist of threats to capture material or, in more complex examples, there may be a threat of mate, accompanied by a threat to a piece. The fork is a simple example of a double attack.

Example A
White to play

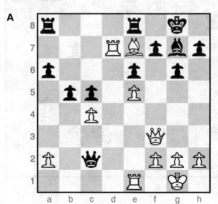

1 Bd8
White breaks the connection between the black rooks and thus creates the dual threats of Qxa8 and Qxf7+.

Example B
White to play

B

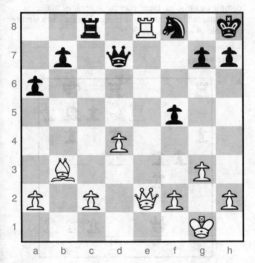

1 Qc4

White threatens a mate on g8 as well as creating an attack against the black rook on c8. If Black replies 1...Rxc4 then 2 Rxf8 is mate.

Example C
White to play

c

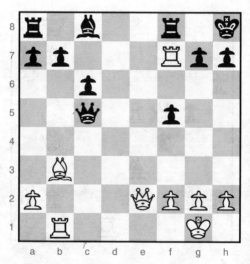

1 Qe5

White creates a double threat of Qxc5 and Qxg7 mate.
If Black tries 1...Qxe5 then 2 Rxf8 is mate.

Example D
Black to play

D

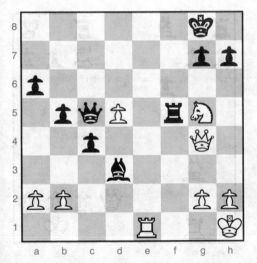

1...Qe3
Black prevents White's impending attack of Re8+,
while simultaneously threatening 2...Qxe1 or 2...Qxg5.
If 2 Rxe3, Rf1 is mate.

DISCOVERED ATTACK

In a discovered attack a piece moves to expose a threat from a piece behind it and meanwhile creates a further threat of its own. The discovered attack is, in effect, a form of double attack.

Example A
Black to play

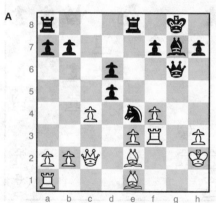

1...Ng5
By moving the knight away, Black uncovers an attack against the unprotected white queen on c2. After 2 Qxg6 Black interposes 2...Nxf3+ before recapturing the queen, and thus wins the exchange.

Example B
White to play

B

1 Rh6
In the diagram, White has a number of tempting
discovered attacks with the rook, but 1 Rh6 is the most
efficient. After 1...Qf8, White finishes with the
attractive combination 2 Rxh7+ Kxh7 3 Qh5 mate.

Example C
White to play

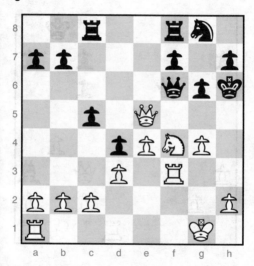

c

1 Ne6

An amazing move! White leaves three pieces *en prise* but Black is unable to successfully capture any of them, e.g. 1...Qxf3 2 Qg5 mate, 1...Qxe5 2 Rh3+ Qh5 3 g5 mate, or 1...Qxe6 2 Rh3 mate.

Example D
Black to play

D

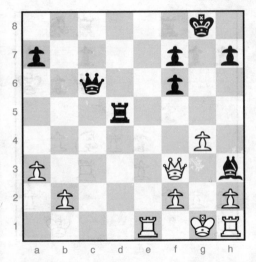

1...Re5

Black uncovers an attack against the white queen while simultaneously threatening the white rook. 2 Qxc6 is met by 2...Rxe1 mate.

DISCOVERED CHECK

A discovered check is a discovered attack where the
primary attacking threat consists of a check to the
opponent's king. A particularly potent form of
discovered check is a double check, where the piece
which moves to clear a line to the opponent's king also
delivers a check itself. A double check can only be met
by moving the king, which can make it a very powerful
attacking weapon.

Example A
White to play

A

1 Qg8+
White lures the black king into the firing line of a
discovered check. 1...Kxg8 2 Be6+ Kh8 3 Rg8 mate. In
this case, White's second move is a double check, a
particularly fearsome device, as the only way to escape
from the check is by moving the king.

Example B
Black to play

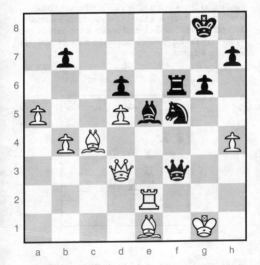

1...Qf1+
A brilliant sacrifice, leading to a neat checkmate after
2 Kxf1 Ne3+ 3 Kg1 Rf1 mate.

Example C

White to play

C

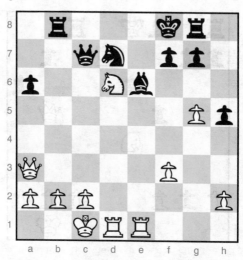

1 Nc8+

White has many tempting discovered checks, but most of them fail to 1...Qc5. However, after 1...Qc5 2 Qxc5+ Nxc5 3 Rd8 is mate, as White's first move has cut off the defence of d8 by the black rook. 1...Nc5 is similarly met by 2 Qxc5+ Qxc5 3 Rd8 mate.

Example D
White to play

D

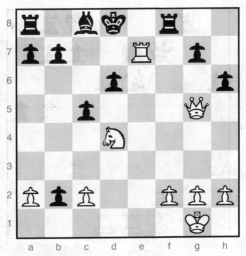

1 Rxb7+

Although White has a discovered check lined up, Black is counterattacking against the white queen, and also has a pawn on b2 which is about to promote. However, White sacrifices the queen to force a neat checkmate: 1...hxg5 2 Nc6+ Ke8 3 Re7 mate.

DEFLECTION

If an opponent's piece is preventing a line of attack which would be favourable if carried out, it may sometimes be possible to deflect the piece from this particular defensive duty. This is often performed with the aid of a sacrifice.

Example A
White to play

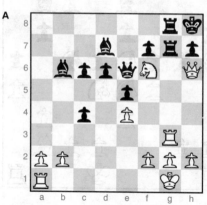

1 Qxh7+

A quick finish. After 1...Rxh7 2 Rxg8 is mate.

Example B
White to play

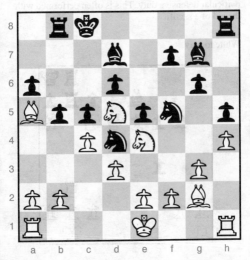

1 Nxd6+

White would like to play Ne7, but the black knight on f5 prevents this. So White deflects the knight and after 1...Nxd6 2 Ne7 is mate.

Example C
White to play

1 Qa4+

White would like to be able to clear the d-file with Nc7+ but, in the diagram position, this is simply met by ...Qxc7. Therefore, White deflects the black queen and after 1...Qxa4 2 Nc7+ Kf8 3 Rxd8 Qe8 4 Rxe8 is mate.

Example D
White to play

D

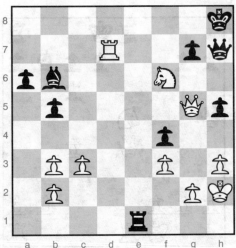

1 Qc5

White would like to play the rook to the back rank, but the bishop on b6 prevents this. White also has to watch out for the Black threat of ...Bg1+ which is why the immediate 1 Nxh7 fails. However, after 1 Qc5 Bxc5 2 Rd8+ mates and, otherwise, 2 Qf8+ will be decisive.

DECOYING

A decoy is a device for luring an opponent's piece to a vulnerable square. This may be a square which blocks an escape route for the king, or perhaps a square where the piece is exposed to capture in the ensuing play.

Example A
White to play

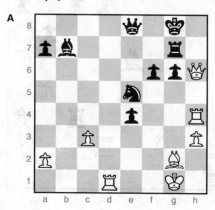

1 Rd8

The immediate move Qh8+ gets White nowhere after 1 ... Kf7. However now, after 1...Qxd8 2 Qh8+ picks up the black queen.

Example B
Black to play

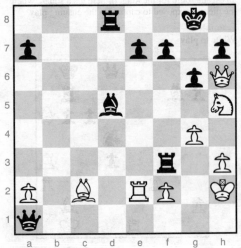

1...Qh1+

Black lures the white king into a deadly double check.

2 Kxh1 Rxh3+ 3 Kg1 Rh1 mate.

Example C
White to play

c

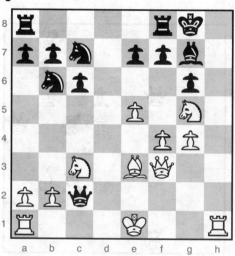

1 Rh8+

It is very tempting to play 1 Qh3 but then Black counters with 1...Rfd8 and White cannot make immediate progress. However, after 1 Rh8+ Bxh8 2 Qh3 creating a flight square for the king with 2...Rfd8 doesn't help, e.g. 3 Qh7+ Kf8 4 Qxh8 mate.

Example D
Black to play

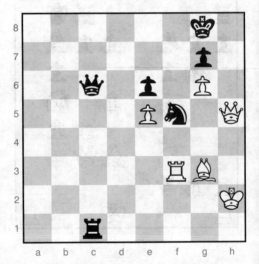

1...Rh1+

Black lures the white king to h1. After 2 Kxh1, the white rook is pinned and 2...Nxg3+ forks the white king and queen.

REMOVING THE DEFENDER

In the earlier section on deflection, we saw how an opponent's piece can often be deflected from a particular defensive task. Instead, it is sometimes possible to simply remove the defending unit by capturing it. This usually involves a sacrifice.

Example A
Black to play

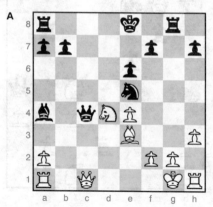

1...Qxd4

The white knight is defending the f3 square. Black therefore removes it and delivers a mating combination 2 Bxd4 Nf3+ 3 Kf1 Bb5+ mating.

Example B
Black to play

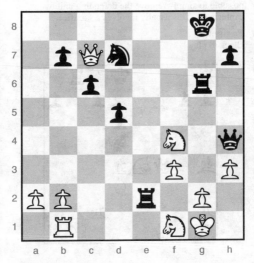

1...Qxf4

The white knight is preventing the black rooks from penetrating into White's camp. Following its removal, mate swiftly follows, e.g. 2 Qxf4 Rexg2+ 3 Kh1 Rg1+ 4 Kh2 R6g2 mate.

Example C
White to play

C

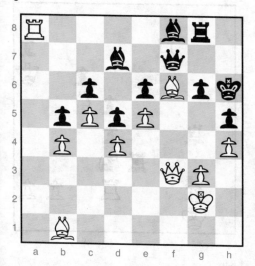

1 Bg5+

White has uncovered an attack against the black queen,
so Black must guard it with 1...Kg7. Now, however, the
guard is removed with 2 Bh6+ and Black loses the
queen.

Example D
White to play

D

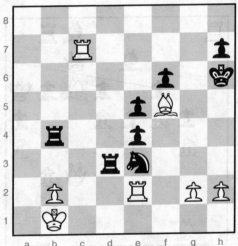

1 Rxe3

White would like to trap the black king in a mating net with h4, but at the moment this would be met by ...Nxf5. So White eliminates the knight and after 1...Rxe3 2 h4, the mate threat of Rxh7 can only be delayed with a few harmless checks.

BLOCKADING

A blockading manoeuvre is used mainly for one of two reasons. Firstly, to oblige an opponent to place a piece on an inconvenient square which blocks an escape route for the king. The second use is to oblige the opponent to block a line or a diagonal on which there existed a potential threat.

Example A
White to play

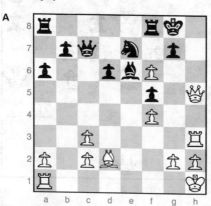

1 f7+

White can give a check along the h-file, but Black simply runs the king to f7. Now, however, the escape route is blocked and Qh8 next move will be checkmate.

Example B
Black to play

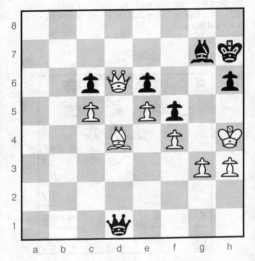

1...Bf6+
A clever move, luring the white e-pawn to f6. After
2 exf6 Kg6 Black threatens ...Qh5 mate and 3 g4 is met
by 3...Qe1 mating. Note that the immediate 1...Kg6
fails to 2 Qxe6+.

Example C
Black to play

C

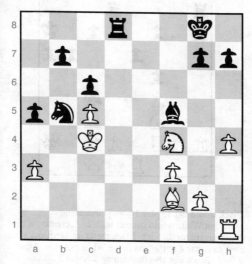

1...Rd3

A beautiful finish. Black threatens ...Rc3 mate, and after 2 Nxd3 Be6 is mate.

Example D
Black to play

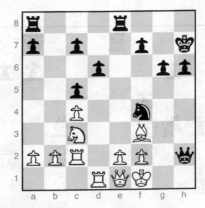

1...Re3

Black would like to play 1...Nh3 threatening ...Qg1 mate, but White would counter with 2 e3, creating a flight square for the king. Black therefore sacrifices a rook to create a traffic jam in the White position. After 2 fxe3 (Black was also threatening ...Rxf3) 2...Nh3 mate is unavoidable.

ADVANCED TACTICS

The following examples are more complex and utilize many of the themes examined in the preceding sections. They demonstrate how these concepts can combine to produce attractive and powerful tactical combinations.

Example A
White to play

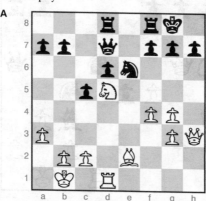

White lures the black queen away from the defence of the kingside and then finishes off with a neat mating combination.

1 Bb5 Qxb5 (1...Qc8 2 Ne7+) 2 Ne7+ Kh8
3 Qxh7+ Kxh7 4 Rh1 mate.

Example B
Black to play

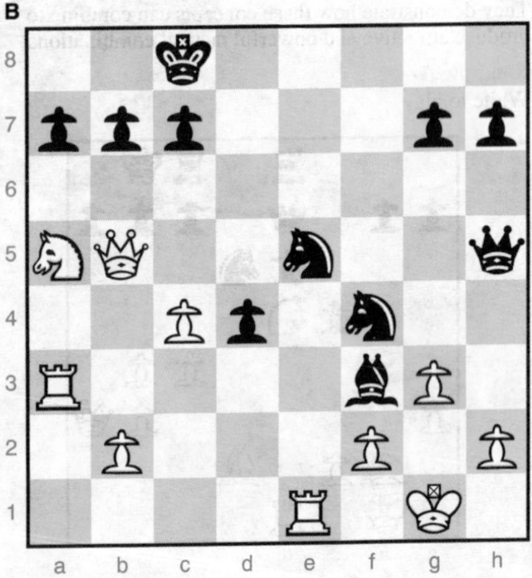

B

An initial queen sacrifice allows the black minor pieces to combine beautifully to deliver checkmate.
1...Qxh2+ 2 Kxh2 Ng4+ 3 Kg1 Nh3+ 4 Kf1 Nh2 mate.

Example C
White to play

C

White blasts a path through to the black king by brute force.
1 Rxg7+ Bxg7 2 Rxg7+ Kh8 3 Rg8+ Kxg8
4 Qg6+ Kh8 5 Qg7 mate.

Example D
White to play

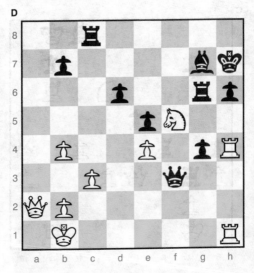

White sacrifices on h6 in order to introduce the queen into the attack. 1 Rxh6+ Rxh6 2 Rxh6+ Bxh6 3 Qf7+ Kh8 4 Qf6+ Kg8 5 Ne7+ Kh7 6 Qg6+ and mate next move. Alternatively, 1...Bxh6 2 Rxh6+ Rxh6 3 Qf7+ and 4 Qg7 mate. Queen and knight can be a very powerful attacking combination.

Example E
White to play

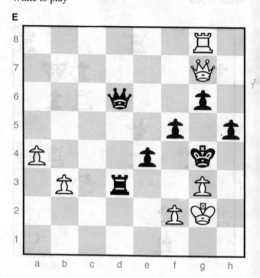

The white pieces have chased Black's king down the kingside, but now he turns the tables and combines with the black queen in an attack against the white king.
1...Rxg3+ 2 fxg3 Qd2+ 3 Kf1 Kf3, and White will soon be mated.

Example F
White to play

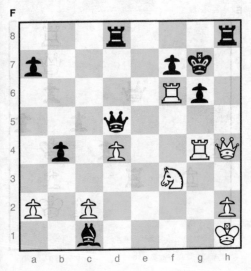

White sacrifices a rook to open up tactical possibilities against the black king.
1 Rfxg6+ fxg6 2 Qe7+ Qf7 (2...Kh6 3 Rh4+ wins the queen or 2...Kg8 3 Rxg6 mate) 3 Rxg6+ Kxg6 4 Ne5+ and White wins the black queen, and will soon deliver mate.

Example G
White to play

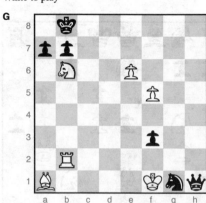

Despite his dangerous passed pawns, White seems to be in trouble, as Black has powerful threats against white's king. However, he finds a clever way to capture the black queen.
1 Rh2 Qxh2 2 Be5+ Qxe5 3 Nd7+ Kc7 4 Nxe5, and now Black must move the knight, when 5 e7 will force a new queen.

Example H
White to play

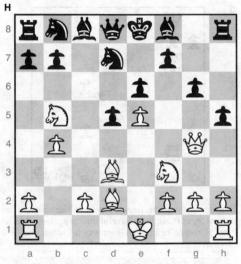

In this position from early in the game, Black has won a pawn, but lost far too much time. White now punishes this extravagance with a beautiful queen sacrifice.
1 Qxe6+ fxe6 2 Bxg6+ Ke7 3 Bg5+ Nf6 4 exf6+ Kd7
5 Ne5 mate.

Example I
White to play

I

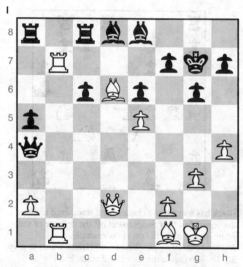

White has seen the possibility to launch a mating attack with a queen sacrifice, but first needs to cut off the black queen's route to the kingside.
1 R1b4 axb4 2 Qh6+ Kxh6 3 Bf8+ Kh5 4 Be2 mate. Note that the immediate 1 Qh6+ fails to 1...Kxh6 2 Bf8+ Kh5 3 Be2 Qg4, hence White's initial rook sacrifice.

Example J
Black to play

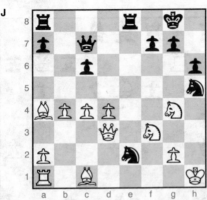

Black has spotted the chance for a smothered mate in
the corner but first needs to cut off the defence of the
white queen, as in the previous example.

1...Nhg3+ 2 Kh2 Nf1+ 3 Kh1 Re3 (Black wants to play
3...Qh2+ to create the smothered mate, but 4 N3xh2
defends by giving the white queen access to g3)

4 Bxe3 Qh2+ (now that the white queen has been cut
off from g3, Black's combination can go ahead)

5 Ngxh2 Nfg3 mate.

4. Opening play

GENERAL PRINCIPLES OF THE OPENINGS

The most important part of the opening strategy for both Black and White is development. This involves:
- Bringing the pieces into play as quickly as possible.
- Controlling the four central squares.

Development
- White always moves first.
- 1 e4 or 1 d4 are very common first moves (Diagram A).
- 1 e4 enables the bishop on f1 and the queen on d1 to develop.
- 1 e4 means the pawn has capturing possibilities on the squares d5 and f5.
- 1 d4 enables the bishop on c1 to develop.
- 1 d4 attacks the c5 and e5 squares.

A

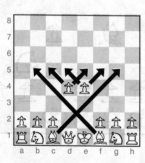

Develop the minor pieces first

Develop the minor pieces first, into the centre, usually knights before bishops. For example:

- Nf3 attacks the e5 and d4 squares.
- Be2, Bc4 or Bb5 (not Bd3, because this prevents the pawn on d2 from advancing).
- the squares f1 and g1 are vacant, so White can castle, getting the king to safety (Diagram B).

B

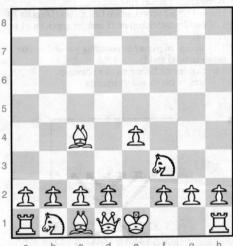

Castle early

Castle early, normally kingside (Diagram C).

- The king is placed in safety behind a row of pawns.
- The king is not left in the centre open to attack.
- A rook is brought into play towards the centre.

C

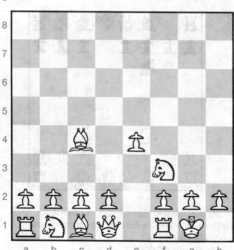

Development is often more important than grabbing pawns

	White	Black		White	Black
1	e4	e5	4	c3	dxc3
2	Nf3	Nc6	5	Nxc3 (Diagram D)
3	d4	exd4			

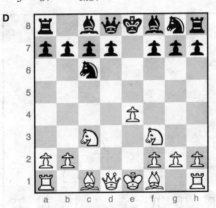

White has 'allowed' himself to be a pawn down.
But look how White's development is much further advanced than Black's.

- Both knights are developed.
- There are open diagonals for both bishops.
- The bishop on f1 can move and then White can castle the king into safety.

Develop positively

	White	Black		White	Black
1	d4	d5	4	Bg5	Be7
2	c4	e6	5	e3	0–0
3	Nc3	Nf6			

E

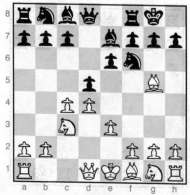

Black must not allow White to dominate the centre.

In Diagram E Black has:

- Brought the king's knight into the centre.
- Castled.
- Is ready to develop the queenside.

Do not move the same piece twice

	White	Black		White	Black
1	e4	e5	5	d4	Nd6
2	Nf3	Nc6	6	Bxc6	bxc6
3	Bb5	Nf6	7	dxe5	Nb7
4	0-0	Nxe4		(Diagram F)	

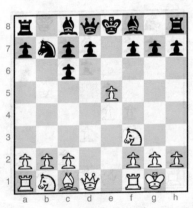

F

Poor development by Black:

- The king's knight has moved four times in the first seven moves.
- The knight on b7 is not concentrating on the centre.
- White has castled.
- White has a pawn in the centre – e5.
- White has easier development.

The game continued:

	White	Black
8	Nd4	Be7
9	Nf5	Bf8

A loss of time; the bishop goes back to where it has come from.

10	Re1	g6
11	Nd6+	Bxd6
12	exd6+	Kf8
13	Bh6+	Kg8
14	Qd4	f6
15	Qc4	mate (Diagram G)

G

Do not bring the queen out too soon

As the queen is such a powerful piece, you may be
tempted to develop it early on. However, this temptation
should be resisted, as the queen will be very vulnerable
to attack by the opponent's minor pieces. Witness the
following example.

	White	Black		White	Black
1	e4	e5	4	d3	Nf6
2	f4	d5	5	dxe4	Nxe4
3	exd5	e4	6	g3?	(Diagram H)

H

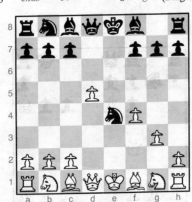

6 Nf3 would have been a better developing move.

	White	Black			White	Black
6	...	Bc5		10	Qxg4	Bf2+
7	Qe2	0–0		11	Ke2	Nf6+
8	Qc4	Qe7		12	Kxf2	Nxg4+
9	Qe2	Bg4			(Diagram I)	

I

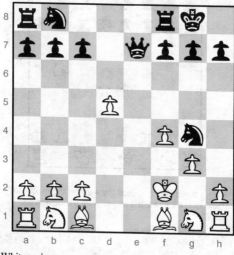

White resigns.

Unnecessary moves

	White	Black		White	Black
1	e4	e5	5	Kf1	Bb6
2	f4	exf4	6	Nf3	Qd8
3	Bc4	Bc5	7	Bxf4	Ne7
4	d4	Qh4+	8	Ng5	0–0
				(Diagram J)	

J

White's pawns have opened the way for the pieces to attack. Black has wasted moves with the bishop and queen.

	White	Black		White	Black
9	Qh5	h6	11	Qxh6+	gxh6
10	Bxf7+	Kh8	12	Be5 mate	
				(Diagram K)	

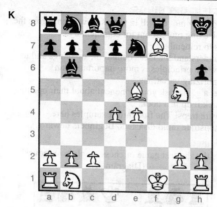

Summary of opening principles and development

- Develop minor pieces first.
- Castle early.
- Do not move the same piece twice or make unnecessary moves.
- Develop positively.
- Do not attack until development is complete.
- Do not grab pawns unnecessarily while developing.
- Aim to control the centre.
- Avoid moves which block in your own pieces.

These principles apply to all games of chess, whether school tournaments, club play or world championships.

SPECIFIC OPENINGS

The opening moves will in places be written across the page, leaving more room for commentary.

Points to remember:

- To understand the ideas behind the openings and to know the principles is more important than memorizing variations.
- After a game, ask your opponent about their opening, or look it up in a book.
- Beware traps! The first three examples here demonstrate rapid disasters. Beginners beware!

Fool's mate

This is the shortest game of chess – only two moves!
1 g4 e5 2 f3 Qh4 mate (Diagram A).

- White has ignored the centre and has not developed.
- The f-pawn move has exposed the king.

Scholar's mate
1 e4 e5 2 Qh5 Nc6 3 Bc4 Bc5 4 Qxf7 mate (Diagram B).

- 3...Bc5 was a bad move.
- Black could have prevented mate by 3...Qe7 or 3...Qf6 or 3...g6 or 3...Nh6.
- Different moves could be played – 2 Qf3 or 2...Nf6.
- Do not ignore dangers to your pieces while developing.

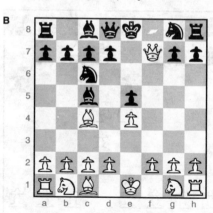

Legall's Legacy

1 e4 e5 2 Nf3 d6 3 Bc4 Bg4 4 Nc3 h6 5 Nxe5 Bxd1
6 Bxf7+ Ke7 7 Nd5 mate (**Diagram C**).

- Black's 4th move did not assist development and is an unnecessary pawn move.
- Look carefully at the whole board while developing.
- Do not develop without watching how your opponent is developing.

C

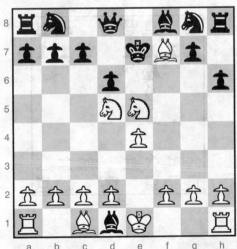

KING PAWN OPENINGS 1e4
Scotch Game

	White	Black
1	e4	e5
2	Nf3	Nc6
3	d4	exd4 (Diagram A)

A

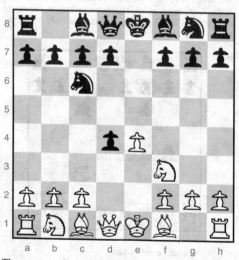

The game continues 4 Nxd4 Nf6 5 Nc3.
This is an open position, good for beginners.

Giuoco Piano (Italian Opening)

	White	Black		White	Black
1	e4	e5	4	c3	Nf6
2	Nf3	Nc6	5	d4	exd4
3	Bc4	Bc5	6	cxd4	Bb4+
				(Diagram B)	

White has developed the king's bishop to c4 and not, as in the Ruy Lopez, to b5. This concentrates on the centre and prevents Black playing ...d5 immediately. White has a strong centre.

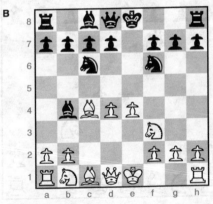

- 7 Bd2 is a safe continuation.
- 7 Nc3 is complicated.

Four Knights' Game

	White	Black
1	e4	e5
2	Nf3	Nc6
3	Nc3	Nf6 (Diagram C)

White develops quickly but is not offering much in the way of potential attack. Black has plenty of room to develop.

C

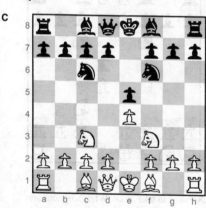

The game continues 4 Bc4 Bc5 5 0–0 0–0.
A solid opening, safe but dull.

Two Knights' Defence

	White	Black
1	e4	e5
2	Nf3	Nc6
3	Bc4	Nf6 (Diagram D)

D

Black threatens to take on e4. White's options are:

- Defend the pawn with 4 d3 or 4 Nc3.
- Counterattack against the f7 pawn with 4 Ng5.
- Continue development while opening up the game with 4 d4 exd4 5 0–0.

Fegatello (Fried Liver)

	White	Black		White	Black
1	e4	e5	4	Ng5	d5
2	Nf3	Nc6	5	exd5	Nxd5
3	Bc4	Nf6	6	Nxf7	

(Diagram E)

E

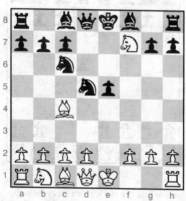

A dangerous gambit by White. After 6...Kxf7 7 Qf3+ Black must defend his knight and so 7...Ke6 is forced. The black king is then in a dangerously exposed position.

King's Gambit

	White	Black
1	e4	e5
2	f4	(Diagram F)

F

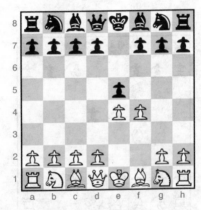

White tries to lure the black pawn away from the centre. The resulting play in this, the oldest of openings, is often very sharp and double-edged. One possible continuation, known as the Muzio Gambit, is 2...exf4 3 Nf3 g5 4 Bc4 g4 5 0–0 gxf3 6 Qxf3. Exciting, but risky for both sides.

Evans' Gambit

	White	Black
1	e4	e5
2	Nf3	Nc6
3	Bc4	Bc5
4	b4	(Diagram G)

G

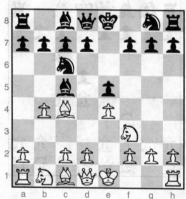

4...Bxb4 5 c3 Bc5 6 d4.

An attempt to inject some life into the 'Quiet Game'–Giuoco Piano.

4 b4 lures the bishop away from the centre so White can develop a strong pawn centre with 5 c3, followed by 6 d4.

Vienna Game

	White	Black
1	e4	e5
2	Nc3	Nf6
3	f4	(Diagram H)

H

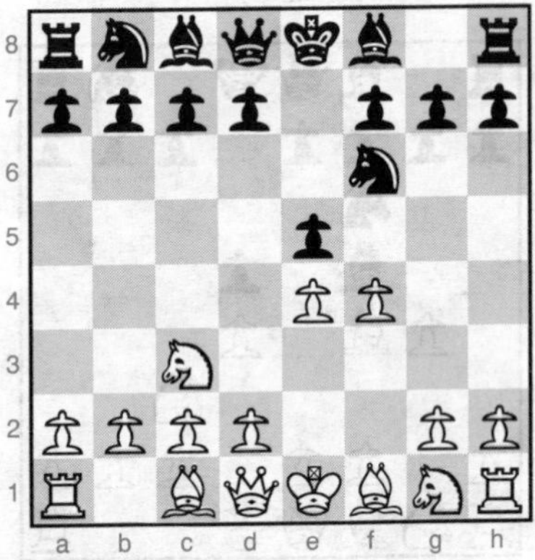

A common continuation is 3...d5 4 fxe5 Nxe4.

If Black plays 3...exf4, then White replies 4 e5, a strong move embarrassing Black's knight.

Danish Gambit

	White	Black		White	Black
1	e4	e5	4	Bc4	cxb2
2	d4	exd4	5	Bxb2	(Diagram I)
3	c3	dxc3			

I

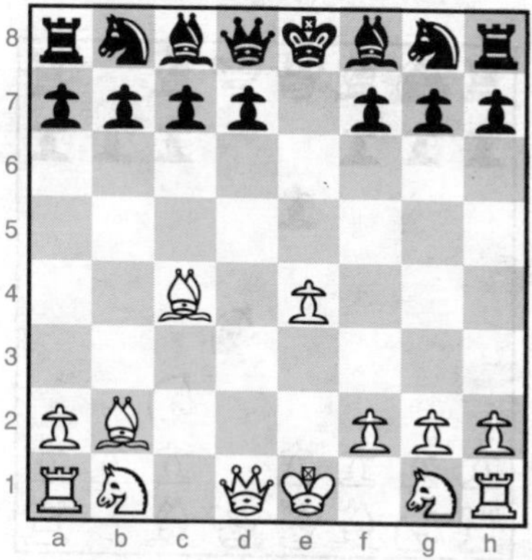

White has sacrificed two pawns in order to create pressure with the two bishops bearing down on Black's kingside.

Petroff Defence (Russian Defence)

	White	Black
1	e4	e5
2	Nf3	Nf6
3	Nxe5	d6
4	Nf3	Nxe4 (Diagram J)

J

A solid opening by Black, attempting to neutralize White's early initiative. Note that Black must not play 3...Nxe4, as after 4 Qe2 Nf6 5 Nc6+ White's discovered check wins the black queen.

Ruy Lopez (Spanish Opening)

	White	Black
1	e4	e5
2	Nf3	Nc6
3	Bb5	(Diagram K)

K

White pressurizes the black e-pawn by creating the possibility of Bxc6 followed by Nxe5. If Black moves the d-pawn, then the knight on c6 is pinned (see p.45). There are a number of Black defences to the Ruy Lopez.

Black defences to the Ruy Lopez
Closed Defence (to the Ruy Lopez)

	White	Black
3	...	a6
4	Ba4	Nf6
5	0–0	Be7
6	Re1	b5
7	Bb3	d6
8	c3	0–0 (Diagram L)

L

White has castled, and his rook is on the e-file. This defence is the most popular.

Marshall Gambit (to the Ruy Lopez)

	White	Black		White	Black
3	...	a6	8	c3	d5
4	Ba4	Nf6	9	exd5	Nxd5
5	0–0	Be7	10	Nxe5	Nxe5
6	Re1	b5	11	Rxe5	c6
7	Bb3	0–0		(Diagram M)	

M

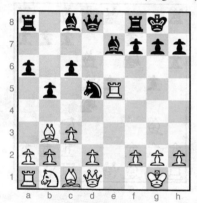

Black has sacrificed a pawn in order to gain a lead in development and the chance of a kingside attack.

Open Defence (to the Ruy Lopez)

	White	Black		White	Black
3	...	a6	7	Bb3	d5
4	Ba4	Nf6	8	dxe5	Be6
5	0–0	Nxe4		(Diagram N)	
6	d4	b5			

N

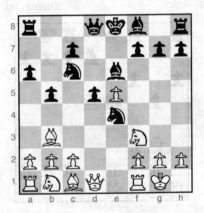

Black has obtained free piece play, at the cost of potential structural weaknesses on the queenside. If Black does not play 3...a6, the Berlin Defence (3...Nf6) or the Classical Defence (3...Bc5) are possibilities.

Berlin Defence (to the Ruy Lopez)

	White	Black			White	Black
3	...	Nf6		7	Bxc6	bxc6
4	0–0	Nxe4		8	dxe5	Nb7
5	d4	Be7			(Diagram O)	
6	Qe2	Nd6				

O

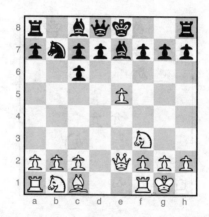

There are other defences where the important move is
...Nf6, attacking the white e-pawn.

Classical Defence (to the Ruy Lopez)

	White	Black
3	...	Bc5
4	c3	Nf6
5	0–0	0–0
6	d4	Bb6 (Diagram P)

P

Early castling by Black and White, but White has two strong pawns in the centre.

Philidor's Defence

	White	Black
1	e4	e5
2	Nf3	d6
3	d4	(Diagram A)

A

Black's e-pawn is supported by another pawn, and not by the queen's knight. This defence prevents White playing the Ruy Lopez, but it leaves the black king's bishop blocked in.

Caro-Kann Defence

	White	Black
1	e4	c6 (Diagram B)

B

With 1...c6, Black intends to follow up with ...d5, placing a pawn in the centre of the board. Supporting this pawn with ...c6 avoids locking in the queen's bishop (compare with the French Defence 1 e4 e6), but deprives the queen's knight of a good development square.

Advance Variation (Caro-Kann Defence)

	White	Black
1	e4	c6
2	d4	d5
3	e5 (Diagram C)	

C

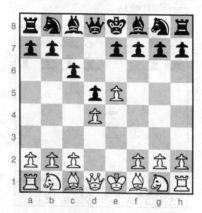

White gains space in the centre and deprives Black of the possibility of developing the king's knight on f6.

Panov-Botvinnik Attack (Caro-Kann Defence)

	White	Black
1	e4	c6
2	d4	d5
3	exd5	cxd5
4	c4 (Diagram D)	

D

White decides on a wide open game with good development possibilities for all the pieces. Black has the opportunity to capture on c4 at some point, which will leave White with an isolated pawn on d4 – a potential source of weakness.

Classical Variation (Caro-Kann Defence)

	White	Black
1	e4	c6
2	d4	d5
3	Nc3	dxe4
4	Nxe4	Nd7 (Diagram E)

E

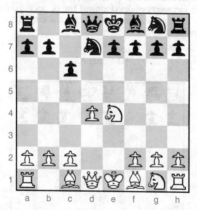

White has an advantage in space and mobility, but Black has a solid position and prepares to challenge the white knight with ...Ngf6.

Sicilian Defence

In the 1840s it was said that '1...c5 is the best answer to
1 e4 as it renders the formation of a centre
impracticable for White and prevents every attack.'
It is today probably the most popular of defences to
1 e4 at club and international level, and it gives Black
aggressive and counterattacking opportunities. It breaks
up the symmetry of development and opens the c-file
early in the game. There is likely to be a kingside v
queenside struggle.

	White	Black
1	e4	c5 (Diagram A)

A

Dragon Variation (Sicilian Defence)

	White	Black
2	Nf3	d6
3	d4	cxd4
4	Nxd4	Nf6
5	Nc3	g6
6	Be3	Bg7 (Diagram B)

B

In this variation Black develops the king's bishop on the long diagonal, instead of one of the more usual squares, such as e7, c5 or b4. This 'long diagonal' development (by either side, on either wing) is known as a fianchetto.

Scheveningen Variation (Sicilian Defence)

	White	Black
2	Nf3	e6
3	d4	cxd4
4	Nxd4	Nf6
5	Nc3	d6 (Diagram C)

C

The black pawns are not advanced beyond the third rank (a small centre). They will advance later when they have support from other pieces.

Taimanov Variation (Sicilian Defence)

	White	Black
2	Nf3	Nc6
3	d4	cxd4
4	Nxd4	e6 (Diagram D)

D

Black leaves the diagonal open for the king's bishop to develop actively on either c5 or b4. The latter case is particularly likely if White develops the queen's knight on c3, when the move ...Bb4 will pin the knight.

Richter-Rauzer Variation (Sicilian Defence)

	White	Black		White	Black
2	Nf3	Nc6	5	Nc3	d6
3	d4	cxd4	6	Bg5 (Diagram E)	
4	Nxd4	Nf6			

E

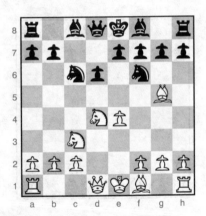

White develops the queen's bishop actively on g5, intending to worry Black with the possibility of capturing the knight on f6. White also plans to continue with Qd2 and 0–0–0, developing quickly.

Najdorf Variation (Sicilian Defence)

	White	Black
2	Nf3	d6
3	d4	cxd4
4	Nxd4	Nf6
5	Nc3	a6 (Diagram F)

F

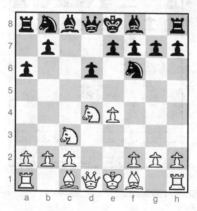

Black's last move prevents a white knight or bishop moving to b5. Later Black can play ...b5.

Closed Variation (Sicilian Defence)

	White	Black
2	Nc3	Nc6 (Diagram G)

G

A possible continuation is 3 g3 g6 4 Bg2 Bg7 5 Nge2 Nf6 6 0–0 0–0.

White deliberately refrains from opening the position early. This leads to a slower, more manoeuvring type of game than in open lines where White plays d4.

Morra Gambit (Sicilian Defence)

	White	Black
2	d4	cxd4
3	c3 (Diagram H)	

H

A possible continuation is 3...dxc3 4 Nxc3 d6 5 Bc4 e6.

A popular gambit at club level, though international players consider it too optimistic.
Black can play safe by declining the gambit with 3...d5.

French Defence

	White	Black
1	e4	e6
2	d4	d5 (Diagram A)

A

Black is staking a claim for the centre with the d-pawn supported by the e-pawn. A solid way to play, the only drawback is the limited scope of the queen's bishop.

Advance Variation (French Defence)

	White	Black
1	e4	e6
2	d4	d5
3	e5 (Diagram B)	

B

A possible continuation is 3...c5 4 c3 Nc6 5 Nf3.

This leads to a blocked pawn position in the centre. White's attacking chances lie mainly on the kingside and Black's on the queenside.

Tarrasch Variation (French Defence)

	White	Black
1	e4	e6
2	d4	d5
3	Nd2 (Diagram C)	

C

A possible continuation is 3...c5 4 exd5 exd5 5 Ngf3 Bd6 6 dxc5 Bxc5.

This leads to an open position where Black has plenty of room to develop the pieces but the isolated pawn (see p. 182) may become a target.

Black can also play 3...Nf6 when White's normal reply 4 e5 leads to a position similar to the Advance Variation.

Exchange Variation (French Defence)

	White	Black
1	e4	e6
2	d4	d5
3	exd5	exd5 (Diagram D)

D

A possible continuation is 4 Nf3 Nf6 5 Bd3 Bd6
6 0–0 0–0.

This leads to a symmetrical pawn formation and is
considered a safe but dull option for White.

Winawer Variation (French Defence)

	White	Black
1	e4	e6
2	d4	d5
3	Nc3	Bb4 (Diagram E)

E

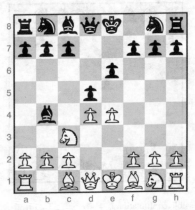

A possible continuation is 4 e5 c5 5 a3 Bxc3+ 6 bxc3.

This produces an unbalanced pawn formation and often leads to exciting games where White attacks on the kingside and Black on the queenside.

Classical Variation (French Defence)

	White	Black
1	e4	e6
2	d4	d5
3	Nc3	Nf6
4	Bg5	(Diagram F)

F

A possible continuation is 4...Be7 5 e5 Nfd7 6 Bxe7 Qxe7.

As in most other variations of the French Defence, White's main prospects lie on the kingside and Black's on the queenside.

Alekhine's Defence

	White	Black
1	e4	Nf6 (Diagram G)

G

This opening appears to contradict good opening
principles, as it allows the knight to be kicked around
the board. A possible continuation is 2 e5 Nd5 3 d4 d6
4 c4 Nb6 5 f4. This looks very good for White, who has
developed a strong centre while gaining time. Black,
however, hopes that White's lack of development will
prove to be a handicap and that the centre will be over-
extended.

Pirc Defence

	White	Black
1	e4	d6
2	d4	Nf6
3	Nc3	g6 (Diagram H)

H

Black plans to develop the king's bishop on g7 and get the king to safety by castling kingside. White has been allowed to dominate the centre in the initial play, but Black intends to counter there later with thrusts such as ...c5 or ...e5.

Modern Defence

	White	Black
1	e4	g6
2	d4	Bg7 (Diagram I)

I

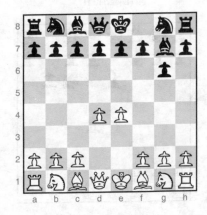

Similar to the Pirc defence, in that Black refrains from challenging in the centre until a later stage. By delaying development on the king's knight, Black keeps extra options open.

Scandinavian Defence

	White	Black
1	e4	d5 (Diagram J)

J

The Scandinavian Defence (also known as Centre Counter Defence) is an unusual opening where, after the continuation 2 exd5 Qxd5, Black's queen comes into play at an early stage. This goes against general principles but Black hopes to gain free play for the pieces.

QUEEN PAWN OPENINGS 1d4

There are basic differences between kingside openings
and queenside openings.

- The white pawn on d4 is already defended by the
  queen.
- 2 c4 does not expose the king, so 2 c4 is more
  common than 2 Nc3.

Queen's Gambit Accepted

	White	Black
1	d4	d5
2	c4	dxc4 (Diagram A)

A

So-called because Black has taken the pawn. White has various possibilities of development, one of which is 3 e4 attacking the c-pawn. A common beginner's mistake is 2...Nf6, because this gives White a strong pawn centre with 3 cxd5 Nxd5 4 e4.

Queen's Gambit Declined

	White	Black
1	d4	d5
2	c4	e6
3	Nc3	Nf6 (Diagram B)

B

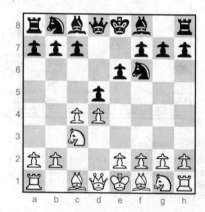

Black's e-pawn supports d5, but the black queen's bishop is temporarily blocked in.

Slav Defence

	White	Black
1	d4	d5
2	c4	c6 (Diagram C)

C

The moves continue 3 Nf3 Nf6 4 Nc3.

Unlike the Queen's Gambit Declined, here Black can develop the queen's bishop. The drawback, however, is that the queen's knight is deprived of its best development square – c6.

King's Indian Defence
Classical Variation (King's Indian Defence)

	White	Black		White	Black
1	d4	Nf6	5	Be2	0–0
2	c4	g6	6	Nf3	e5
3	Nc3	Bg7		(Diagram D)	
4	e4	d6			

D

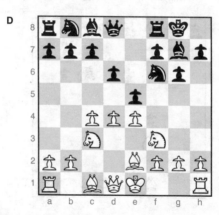

White has three pawns in the centre which Black will try to attack. It looks as if Black has to lose a pawn on e5. But after 7 dxe5 dxe5 8 Qxd8 Rxd8 9 Nxe5 Nxe4, the black bishop threatens the advanced white knight.

Sämisch Variation (King's Indian Defence)

	White	Black
1	d4	Nf6
2	c4	g6
3	Nc3	Bg7
4	e4	d6
5	f3 (Diagram E)	

E

White has a strong pawn centre but Black has more pieces developed. White often castles queenside and both sides then attack each other's king.

Four Pawns Attack (King's Indian Defence)

	White	Black
1	d4	Nf6
2	c4	g6
3	Nc3	Bg7
4	e4	d6
5	f4 (Diagram F)	

F

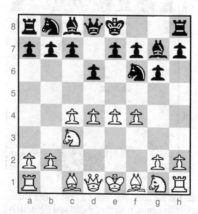

White has created a large centre, but it is not yet supported by pieces. Black has the better development and is ready to castle. A dangerous variation for both sides!

Grünfeld Defence

	White	Black
1	d4	Nf6
2	c4	g6
3	Nc3	d5 (Diagram G)

G

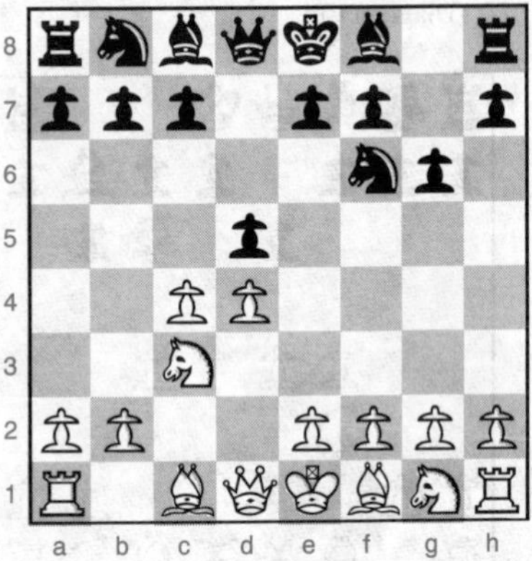

White has set up a strong pawn centre. But Black attacks this centre with the bishop and eventually the c-pawn. A possible combination is:
4 cxd5 Nxd5 5 e4 Nxc3 6 bxc3 Bg7 7 Nf3 c5.

Nimzo Indian Defence

	White	Black
1	d4	Nf6
2	c4	e6
3	Nc3	Bb4 (Diagram H)

H

Black has pinned the white knight on c3, so that:
- Black controls e4.
- Black prevents White from placing three connected pawns in the centre, as in the King's Indian Defence.
- The most popular reply for White is 4 e3.
- Other well-known replies are 4 a3, 4 Qc2, 4 Bg5.

The simplest continuation 4 e3 (Nimzo Indian Defence)

	White	Black
1	d4	Nf6
2	c4	e6
3	Nc3	Bb4
4	e3 (Diagram I)	

I

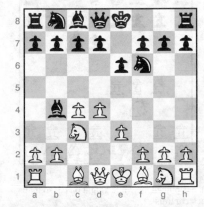

White supports the centre and frees lines for the pieces to develop. Black can either capture on c3 and try to exploit the resultant doubled white c-pawns, or counter in the centre with moves such as ...c5 or ...d5.

Classical Variation (Nimzo Indian Defence)

	White	Black
1	d4	Nf6
2	c4	e6
3	Nc3	Bb4
4	Qc2 (Diagram J)	

J

White lends extra support to the knight on c3 and prevents the possibility of doubled pawns arising on the c-file.

Leningrad Variation (Nimzo Indian Defence)

	White	Black
1	d4	Nf6
2	c4	e6
3	Nc3	Bb4
4	Bg5 (Diagram K)	

K

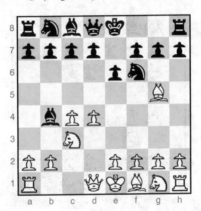

White counters the pin on the queen's knight with a pin against the opposing knight on f6. This variation can lead to highly complex play.

Sämisch Variation (Nimzo Indian Defence)

	White	Black
1	d4	Nf6
2	c4	e6
3	Nc3	Bb4
4	f3 (Diagram L)	

L

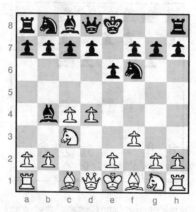

This approach is based on brute force. White intends to continue with e4, forming a large and solid centre. However, the move takes away the best square from the king's knight and does little for White's development. Black should look to counter quickly in the centre.

Queen's Indian Defence

	White	Black
1	d4	Nf6
2	c4	e6
3	Nf3	b6 (Diagram M)

M

Black is ready to fianchetto the queen's bishop and control the important e4 square, already attacked by the king's knight.

Modern Benoni Defence

	White	Black		White	Black
1	d4	Nf6	4	Nc3	exd5
2	c4	c5	5	cxd5	d6
3	d5	e6		(Diagram N)	

N

White has gained space in the centre thanks to the advanced d5 pawn. White will follow up with e4 and gain easy development. Black plans to fianchetto the king's bishop on g7 and will gain play by advancing the queenside pawns.

Dutch Defence

	White	Black
1	d4	f5 (Diagram O)

O

This is another way for Black to attack the important e4 square, but this move does not help Black's development and may lead to weaknesses on the kingside.

Dutch Stonewall

	White	Black		White	Black
1	d4	f5	5	Nf3	0–0
2	c4	e6	6	0–0	d5
3	g3	Nf6		(Diagram P)	
4	Bg2	Be7			

P

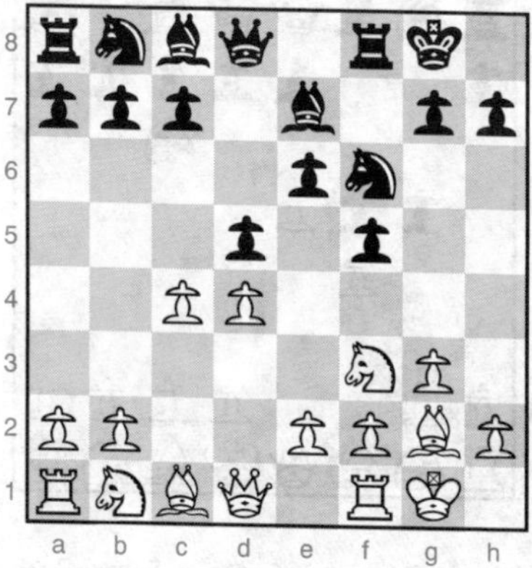

Black has good control of the e4 square, but the black
queen's bishop is blocked in and the e5 square is weak.

Benko Gambit

	White	Black
1	d4	Nf6
2	c4	c5
3	d5	b5 (Diagram Q)

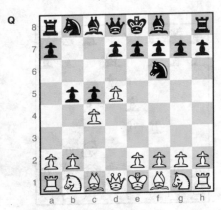

A possible continuation is 4 cxb5 a6 5 bxa6 Bxa6 6 Nc3 d6.

Black has sacrificed a pawn but, in return, has attacking chances on the open files on the queenside. Beginners may find Black's sacrifice surprising, but the gambit is popular at both club and international level.

FLANK OPENINGS

Flank openings exhibit the following features:

- White does not immediately advance either the d- or e-pawn.
- Instead White attacks the centre from the wings, often with a fianchettoed bishop.

Bird's Opening

White moves 1 f4 (Diagram A).

A

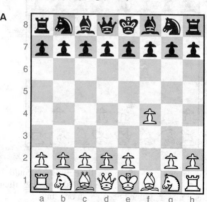

This prevents Black from playing ...e5. Bird said in 1873, 'Having forgotten familiar openings, I commenced adopting f4 for the first move and, finding it led to highly interesting games out of the usual groove, I became partial to it.'

English Opening

White moves 1 c4 (Diagram B).

B

White is covering the d5 square. In reply Black could play 1...e5, 1...c5 or 1...Nf6. The English Opening often transposes into mainline queen pawn openings.

Réti Opening

	White	Black
1	Nf3	d5
2	c4 (Diagram C)	

C

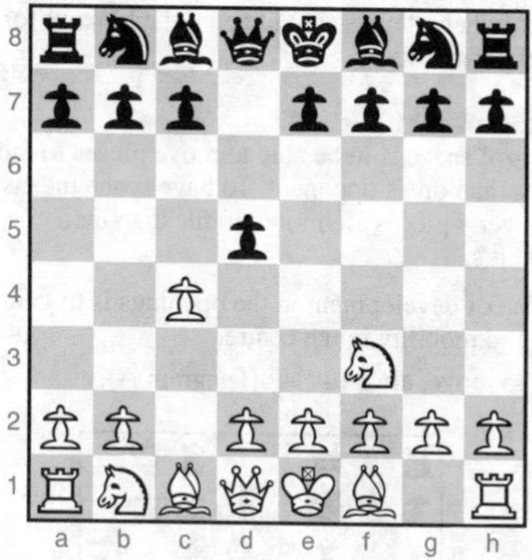

White plans to control the centre without occupying it. Possible plans include developing the bishops on g2 and b2, and delaying the advance of the central pawns until Black's intentions are clear.

5. Middlegame play

The middlegame can be said to start when both players have completed the initial development of their pieces. This is the stage when the two armies come into contact, when players should be on the lookout for tactical possibilities.

SPACE AND MOBILITY

To control space is to be able to move pieces to more squares than one's opponent. To have space means that one player's pieces are more mobile than their opponent's.

The idea of development in the openings is to gain space and mobility in the centre.

Black to move, after 13 Qc2 (Diagram A).

A

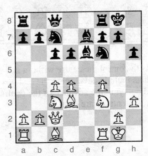

White has an advantage on space and thus wants to avoid exchanges. White has three pawns on the fourth rank, and two knights and a bishop on the third rank. In comparison Black is a little cramped.

We join the following game after Black's 25th move (Diagram B).

B

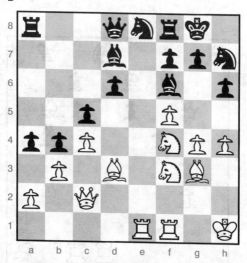

Both players have the same number of pieces. Black has space on the queenside but can't use it to gain an advantage. But White has mobility on the kingside, and this leads to the possibility of a combination.

	White	Black		White	Black
26	Ne6	axb2	31	Qh2	Kg8
27	axb2	Qb6	32	Nxg5	Bxg5
28	Nxf8	Kxf8	33	f6	g6
29	g5	hxg5	34	Bxg6	resigns
30	hxg5	Nxg5		(Diagram C)	

C

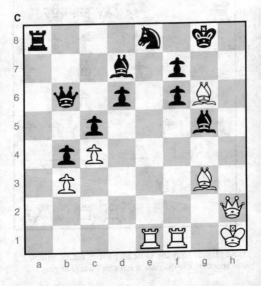

PAWNS IN THE OPENING AND MIDDLEGAME

Pawns in an Open Game

	White	Black			White	Black
1	e4	e5		6	Nxc6	bxc6
2	Nf3	Nc6		7	Bb3	d5
3	d4	exd4		8	exd5	cxd5
4	Nxd4	Nf6			(Diagram A)	
5	Nc3	Bb4				

A

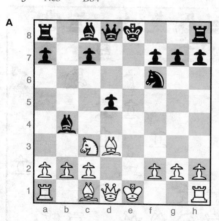

In an open game or position, as above, the pawns are fluid, are able to advance, and many have already been exchanged. Both Black and White are ready to castle, and there will be open lines for rooks and bishops.

Pawns in a Closed Game

In a closed position the central pawns are interlocked in such a way that they cannot be exchanged. There are no open files for the rooks or bishops. In such positions the knight can become relatively more important because of its ability to manoeuvre (see Diagram B).

B

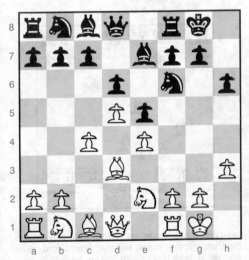

Pawns in the opening

Development may be slowed down by:
- Too many pawn moves.
- Moving a pawn to the wrong square.

	White	Black
1	e4	e5
2	Nf3	f6
3	Bc4	a6
4	0-0 (Diagram C)	

C

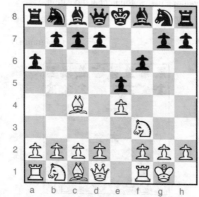

White has developed two minor pieces, and has castled.

Black has made three pawn moves, has not moved a minor piece, and has placed a pawn on f6 which prevents the king's knight from moving there.

One of 4...Nc6 or 4...d6 is essential for Black, because 5 Nxe5 could cause Black some problems. But 5 d4 helps control the centre for White.

Gambit Play

A gambit is one in which material – usually one or more pawns – has been sacrificed (or given up) to gain an advantage in development and position.

	White	Black		White	Black
1	e4	e5	3	c3	
2	d4	exd4		(Diagram D)	

D

White has open diagonals for both bishops.
Other gambits can be found on pages 117-9, 121, 125, 141, 152-3, 168.

PAWN FORMATION

Most openings and defences try to keep the pawns united, so that they guard each other. This is important for the middlegame, and of great value in the endgame (see p.185).

Here is a possible formation after a few moves of the Ruy Lopez (Diagram A).

A

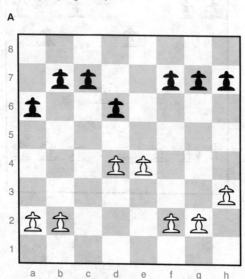

Here is a possible pawn formation in the Sicilian Dragon Variation (Diagram B).

B

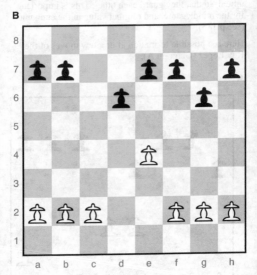

TYPICAL PAWN STRUCTURES
Doubled pawns
Diagram C shows a possible White pawn structure after a few moves.

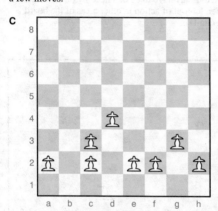

The pawn on c2 has limited power because it cannot move. Doubled pawns usually imply that open files are available. In the above diagram, for example, White may be able to gain useful play on the b-file with a rook.

Isolated pawns

The pawn on h3 is isolated because there are no pawns of the same colour on adjoining files. If attacked it may have to be defended by pieces which are then left out of action in other areas of the board (Diagram D).

D

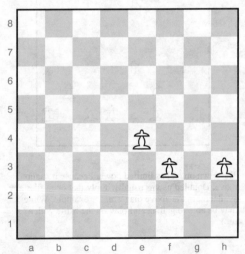

Backward pawns

In Diagram E the white pawn on f3 is a backward pawn as it is unable to advance without being captured by the black pawn at e5. This means that, in certain circumstances, the single black pawn can almost be as valuable as the two white pawns.

E

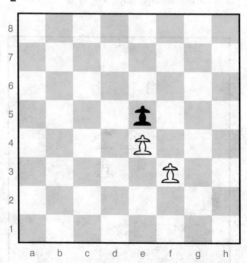

Passed Pawns

In Diagram F the white pawn on d5 is passed, as there are no opposing pawns, either on the same file or adjacent files, between its current position and its queening square (d8). If, for example, there was a black pawn on c7, this would hinder the advance of the white d-pawn and it would not be a passed pawn. Passed pawns can become especially strong in the endgame.

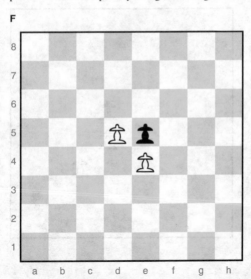

6. Endgame play

INTRODUCTION

Characteristics

An endgame has one or more of the following characteristics:

- There are few pieces on the board, so checkmate is impossible or very difficult.
- There are few or no pawns on the board.
- One side will need to promote a pawn before expecting to checkmate.

Advice

- This final part of the game is as important as the opening and middlegame.
- Bad endgame play can lose or draw a 'won' game.
- Pressure of time and/or tiredness can cause careless moves that spell defeat.
- There are certain techniques (such as a king + pawn v king or king + queen v king) which should be learnt.
- Very careful counting is needed for promotion.
- In the endgame the king does not need to be protected as there is little danger of checkmate. In fact, the king becomes a valuable attacking piece.
- In general, endgames become easier to win as more pieces are exchanged, but more difficult as more pawns are exchanged. Therefore, if you are a pawn up, try to exchange pieces. If you are a pawn down, try to exchange pawns.

BASIC MATES
King and queen v king

This is one of the common endings among beginners, especially after a pawn has been promoted to a queen.

- The player with king and queen must avoid the possibilty of stalemate.
- White must drive Black's king to one of the edges of the board (Diagram A).
- The white king must assist the queen in this movement.

A

If played correctly, this should not take more than 10 moves. Practise this!

	White	Black		White	Black
1	Kb2	Kd5	6	Qg4	Ke1
2	Kc3	Ke5	7	Qg2	Kd1
3	Qg6	Kf4	8	Kd3	Kc1
4	Kd4	Kf3	9	Qc2 mate	
5	Qg5	Kf2		(Diagram B)	

B

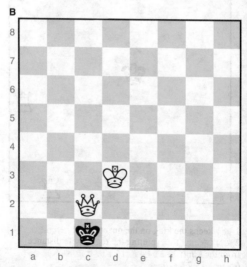

King and two rooks v king

The white king is not needed for the mate.

Position the rooks to force the black king to the edge of the board (Diagram C).

C

1 Re1 keeps the king on the queenside. 1...Kd6
2 Rd4+ Kc5 3 Rd8 (putting the rook a safe distance
from the king) 3...Kc4 4 Rc1+ Kb3 5 Rb8+ Ka2
6 Rb7 Ka3 7 Ra1 mate.

King and rook v king

The black king must be driven to one of the corners of the board, but because the rook is not as strong as the queen, it takes longer to mate the king.

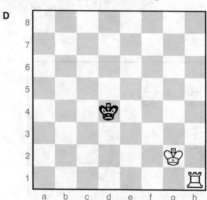

If played correctly, it should take no longer than 16 moves. From Diagram D the moves are:

	White	Black
1	Re1	Kd5
2	Kf3	Kd4
3	Kf4	Kd5
4	Re4	

Black can now only move in a quarter of the board.

	White	Black		White	Black
4	...	Kd6	11	Kd6	Kb7
5	Re5	Kc6	12	Rb5+	Ka6
6	Ke4	Kd6	13	Kc6	Ka7
7	Kd4	Kc6	14	Kc7	Ka6
8	Rd5	Kb6	15	Rc5	Ka7
9	Rc5	Kb7	16	Ra5 mate	
10	Kd5	Kb6		(Diagram E)	

E

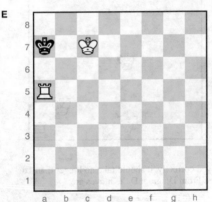

This, too, needs study. Place a black king, white king and white rook in different positions from those above and practise.

The opposition

The opposition is of vital importance in king and pawn endgames. Note the following points:

- Having the opposition enables a player to advance into the opponent's position, perhaps to help a pawn advance and become a queen or to capture the opponent's pawns.
- In Diagram F, the side not having to move has the opposition.

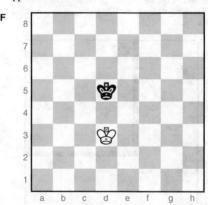

If it is Black to play then 1...Ke5 allows 2 Kc4 and 1...Kc5 allows 2 Ke4. In either case, the white king is able to advance.

KING AND PAWN ENDINGS

The square or queening square

To find out if the king can capture an advancing pawn before it promotes:

- Count the number of squares the pawn has to move forward, including the square it is on.
- Then make a square of that number. This is also known as the quadrant.

In Diagram A the square is within the d-file and 4th rank. The king will capture the pawn, even if it is White to move.

A

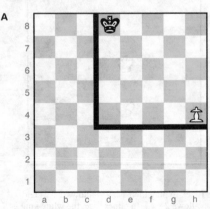

In Diagram B:
- White to move, and the pawn reaches h8 (queening square) because the king is outside the square.
- Black to move plays 1...Kd6. Now the king is inside the square, and therefore captures the pawn if it advances to h8.

B

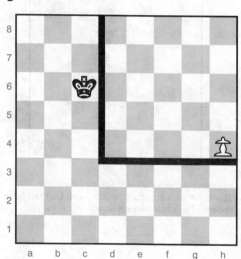

King and two pawns v king

In Diagram C Black is unable to capture on e5 as
1...Kxe5 allows 2 d7 and the white pawn promotes.
Black can only mark time while the white king
advances to shepherd a pawn home.

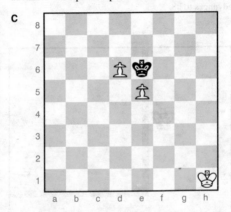

King and pawn on seventh rank v king

This is the most important position in all king and pawn
endings. The result depends on who it is to move.

In Diagram D Black to play loses because the only legal move is 1...Kb7, allowing 2 Kd7 followed by the promotion of the pawn.

White to play only draws because he has the unhappy choice between 1 Kc6, which is stalemate, and any other king move which unguards the pawn on c7 and allows Black to take it.

D

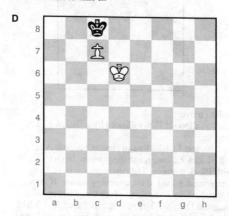

All other king and pawn v king endings depend on whether White can force the position in the diagram with Black to move.

King and pawn on sixth rank v king
This position should be drawn whoever it is to move.
But Black must be very careful (Diagram E).

E

Black to move:

- 1...Kb6 allows 2 Kd6 followed by 3 Kd7, 4 c7 and 5 c8/Q.
- 1...Kb8 and 1...Kd8 lose in similar fashion. After 2 Kd6 Kc8 3 c7 we reach the position in Diagram D with Black to move. The correct move is 1...Kc8, retreating the king to the queening square. If then 2 Kd6 Kd8 3 c7+ Kc8, we reach the position in Diagram D with White to move. If 2 Kc5 Kc7 3 Kb5 Black again retreats 3...Kc8 and White has made no progress.

White to move:

- 1 Kc5 (otherwise White loses the pawn) 1...Kc8 and the position is drawn as shown above. This is the only good move to make.

King and pawn on fifth rank v king
With the pawn on the fifth rank, White can only win if
the king can get in front of the pawn (Diagram F).

F

If it is Black to move in the diagram, this is prevented
by 1...Kc7, when White has nothing better than 2 c6
leading to the drawn position in Diagram E.

White to move can win either by 1 Kc6 (gaining the
opposition) 1...Kb8 2 Kd7, followed by the advance of
the pawn, or by 1 Kd6 Kd8 2 c6 Kc8 3 c7, leading to
Diagram D (see p.195) with Black to move.

King and pawn on fourth rank v king

With the pawn on the fourth rank White can only win if he can get his king in front of the pawn and gain the opposition (Diagram G).

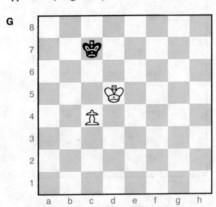

In the diagram, Black to play can gain the opposition by 1...Kd7, when White can make progress neither by 2 Kc5 Kc7 3 Kb5 Kb7, etc., nor 2 c5 leading to the drawn position considered on the previous pages.

White to play wins by 1 Kc5 (not 1 c5, a common beginner's mistake). Now White has the opposition and so Black has to allow the king to advance to the sixth rank, with a win for White as shown in Diagram F (see p.197).

King and h-pawn (or a-pawn) v king
The rules given on the previous pages apply if White has a pawn on any of the files b to g. But the position is drawn if White has an a- or h-pawn (Diagram H).

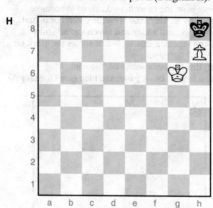

When the pawn reaches the seventh rank it does not matter who it is to move.
If it is White to move, the position will be drawn as in the case of the centre pawn.
If it is Black to move, the position will be stalemate.

Queen v pawn on the seventh rank

In order to handle pawn endgames accurately, it is essential to know the rules concerning the endgame of queen v pawn on the seventh rank.

If a pawn is on the seventh rank, about to promote, supported by its king, and is on the central or b- and g-files, the opponent's king and queen should still win:

- Through repeated checks, White forces the black king in front of the pawn.
- When this has been achieved, the white king approaches the black pawn and king (see Diagram A).

A

The moves are:

	White	Black			White	Black
1	Qe7+	Kf2		4	Qd4+	Ke2
2	Qd6	Ke2		5	Qe4+	Kf2
3	Qe5+	Kf2		6	Qd3	Ke1

The moves 7 Qe3+ Kd1 force the black king in front of the pawn, so the white king moves one square nearer.

	White	Black		White	Black
8	Kb7	Kc2	17	Qe3+	Kd1
9	Qe2	Kc1	18	Kd5	Kc2
10	Qc4+	Kb2	19	Qe2	Kc1
11	Qd3	Kc1	20	Qc4+	Kb2
12	Qc3+	Kd1	21	Qd3	Kc1
13	Kc6	Ke2	22	Qc3+	Kd1
14	Qc2	Ke1	23	Ke4	Ke2
15	Qe4+	Kf2	24	Qe3+	Kd1
16	Qd3	Ke1	25	Kd3	

So the white king has arrived, the pawn is captured and the king and queen eventually mate the black king.

None of the above would have been possible if, in the initial position, the white king had been on e5, e6 or e7, because then White would not have been able to give check.

But the result is different if the pawn is on the c- or f-file (see Diagram B).

B

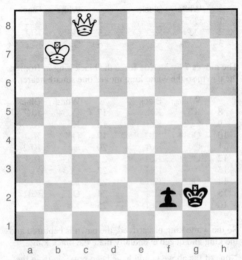

The moves are:

	White	Black
1	Qg4+	Kh2
2	Qf4+	Kg1
3	Qg3+	Kh1

If now 4 Qxf2, then stalemate results.

The result is again different with an a- or h-pawn (Diagram C). The queen approaches step by step.

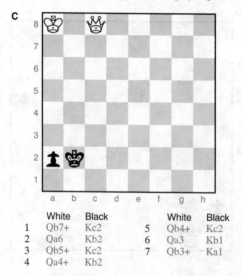

	White	Black		White	Black
1	Qb7+	Kc2	5	Qb4+	Kc2
2	Qa6	Kb2	6	Qa3	Kb1
3	Qb5+	Kc2	7	Qb3+	Ka1
4	Qa4+	Kb2			

The black king is in front of the pawn, but the white king cannot move. If it does, then stalemate results. If the queen moves then the black king moves to b1 or b2.

However, if the white king is nearer the scene of the
action, White may still be able to win (Diagram D).

D

Here the kings are nearer each other than in the
previous diagram. The moves are:

	White	Black		White	Black
1	Qb4+	Ka1	3	Kd3	a1/Q
2	Qc3+	Kb1	4	Qc2 mate	

Outside passed pawns

An outside passed pawn is of great use in acting as a decoy to lure the opposing king away from the defence of its pawns.

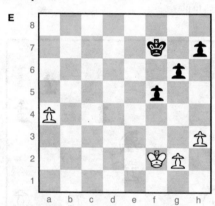

The black king has to move over to the queenside to stop the white a-pawn from promoting. Meanwhile, the white king advances, and captures, the black kingside pawns. White promotes, Black loses:

	White	Black		White	Black
1	...	Ke6	3	a5	Kd5
2	Ke3	Ke5	4	Kf4	

The white king is now onto the black pawns.

FURTHER ENDGAME TACTICS

The king in the endgame

Centralize the king and/or bring the king into the
opponent's camp as soon as possible. In Diagram A it
is Black to play.

A

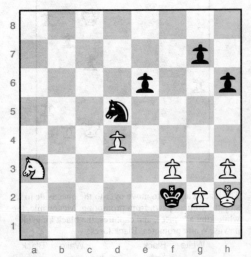

Black is a pawn down, but his king is attacking and the
white king is passive. Black wins as follows:

	White	Black		White	Black
1	...	Ne3	8	Ne1	g3+
2	f4	Nxg2	9	Kh1	Kxe1
3	f5	exf5	10	d7	Kf2
4	d5	Nf4	11	d8/Q	g2+
5	d6	g5	12	Kh2	g1/Q mate
6	Nc2	g4		(Diagram B)	
7	hxg4	fxg4			

B

Stalemate example
In Diagram C Black has material superiority and
clearly the possibility of a win.

C

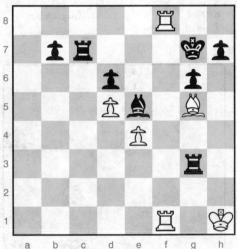

The game continues:

	White	Black		White	Black
1	...	Rxg5	3	Rxf7+	Kxf7
2	R1f7+	Rxf7		(Diagram D)	

D

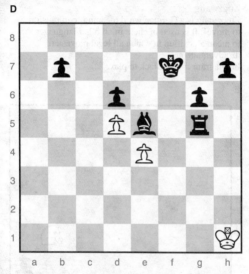

It is now White to move. Black has blundered! White can only move into check from the rook or bishop. There is no legal move for White. The game is a stalemate, which is a draw.

Zugzwang

Zugzwang is a German word meaning 'compulsion to move'. It is used in chess in all other languages to mean a position in which all legal moves are disadvantageous.

In Diagram E it is Black to play.

E

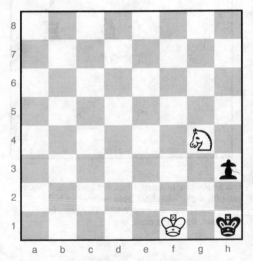

Black can only play 1...h2 and allow 2 Nf2 mate.

Rooks belong behind passed pawns

In Diagram F White's best winning try is 1 Ra1, placing the rook behind the passed pawn. After 1 a7 Black could defend by 1...Ra2, and this move would also be the best try if it were Black to move in the original position.

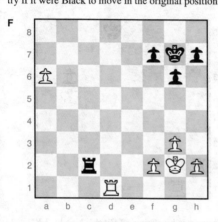

After 1 Ra1 Black will be forced to block the pawn by placing the rook on the passive square a8. In the long run, it will prove impossible to prevent the advance of the white king. But after 1 a7 Ra2 the black rook remains active and will be able to keep White's king at bay.

Building a bridge

In Diagram G Black to move would draw by 1...Kf8, heading for the queening square. White can make no progress, e.g. 2 Kf6 Rf2+ or 2 Rb8+ Kg7 3 Rb7+ Kg8 4 Kf6 Rf2+.

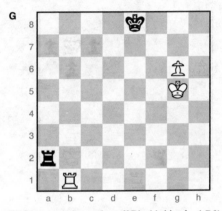

G

White can win by cutting off Black's king by 1 Rf1. Black now cannot prevent the white king from shepherding the pawn home, 1...Rg2+ 2 Kh6 Rh2+ 3 Kg7 Rg2 4 Kh7 Rh2+ 5 Kg8 Rh3 6 g7 Rh2. Now White wins by a technique known as building a bridge, i.e., 7 Rf4 Rh1 8 Re4+ Kd7 9 Kf7 Rf1+ 10 Kg6 Rg1+ 11 Kf6 Rf1+ 12 Kg5 Rg1+ 13 Rg4 and the pawn queens. White's 13th move demonstrates why White must bring the rook to the 4th rank on the 7th move.

Breakthrough

In Diagram H White is to play. The white king is
further away from the pawns than the black king. But
the white pawns are so far advanced that 1 g6 wins!
1...hxg6 2 f6 gxf6 3 h6 and promotes. Or 1...fxg6
2 h6 gxh6 3 f6 and promotes.

H

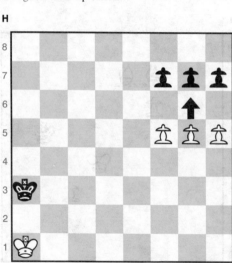

Bishops of the opposite colour

Frequently in endgames, draws are the result of bishops not being able to attack the squares the pawns want to move to. In Diagram I, White, although two pawns up, cannot control the squares c7 and f4, and so the game should end in a draw.

I

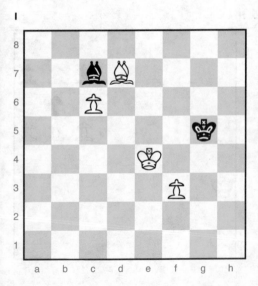

Bishop with a- or h-pawn

White to move in Diagram J. The black king cannot take the pawn defended by the bishop. White wins as follows: 1 Kb8 Kb5 2 Kb7 and the pawn promotes.

Black to move in Diagram J. Neither the white king nor the bishop can drive the black king away from a8, the queening square. 1...Ka7 2 Bb6+ Ka8. If the white king moves, then the black king alternates between a8 and b7, or there is a stalemate. Despite having an extra piece and pawn, White cannot win and the game is drawn.

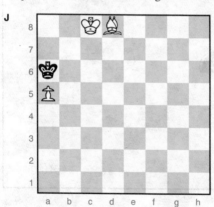

Bishop v knight
Example 1
It is important in these endings that the knight should
not be rendered immobile or 'fettered' (Diagram K).

K

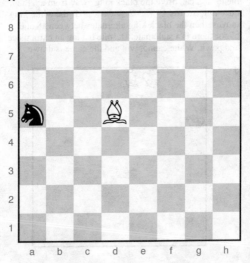

The knight cannot move without being taken (on
squares b3, c4, c6 and b7).

Example 2

In the position in Diagram L, the result depends on whose move it is.

L

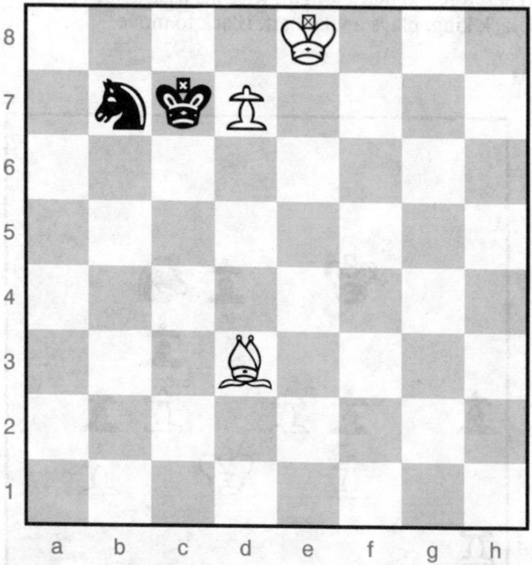

Black to move: 1...Nd6+ 2 Ke7 Nc8+ 3 Ke8 Nd6+. A draw results because the white king is in an unfavourable position.

White to move: 1 Ke7 Nd8 2 Be4 Nf7 3 Bf3 Nd8 4 Bd5. Now Black is in zugzwang, and White wins.

Example 3

The pawns in the position in Diagram M are blocked, and the white pawns are on the same colour as the white bishop, thus hampering the bishop's movement. Therefore the black knight, with the assistance of the black king, plays a vital part. Black to move.

M

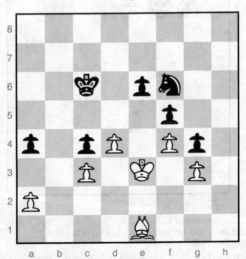

Opposition example

In Diagram N Black has made a breakthrough with the king and now has the opposition. White to move.

N

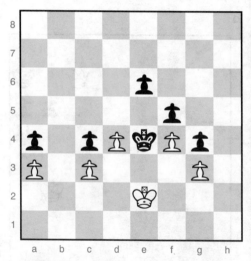

White has to move the king, so the black king reaches either d3 or f3.

Perpetual check

In Diagram O Black is up in material, so White can only hope for a draw. The black king has to move 1...Kh8 then 2 Qf8+ Kh7 3 Qf7+, etc., and this perpetual check is a draw.

O

7. Glossary

Back rank The first rank of Black or White.

Back row The first rank of Black and White (see p.9).

Backward pawn
  i Not guarded by another pawn.
  ii Cannot be advanced with the support of pawns on
  adjacent files.
  iii Is not blocked by an opposition pawn on the same
  file (see p.183).

Blockading Obliging your opponent to block an escape
route or line of potential threat (see p.85).

Castling A combined move of the king and one rook
(see p.32).

Check The king is attacked (see p.52).

Checkmate The king cannot move out of check
(see p.52).

Combination A series of moves which achieve a
specific task, often involving a sacrifice (see p.60).

Decoy A device to lure an opponent's piece to a
vulnerable square (see p.77).

Defender, removing the Capturing a piece by
deflection, usually involving a sacrifice (see p.81).

Deflection The moving of a piece to open a gap (by
deflection) in your opponents defence (see p.73).

Development To move pieces onto squares where they
are active early in the game (see p.99).

Diagonals Squares in a diagonal line, such as a1 to h8.

Discovered attack A piece moves to expose a threat
from a piece behind it (see p.65).

Discovered check An attack upon the king when

another piece in the same line has been moved out of the way (see p.54, 69).

Double attack The creation of two simultaneous threats (see p.61).

Doubled pawns Two pawns on the same file (see p.181).

Endgame The last part of the game when there are few pieces on the board (see p.185).

En passant A special kind of pawn-capturing move (see p.24).

En prise A piece (apart from the king) under attack (see p.67).

Escape square An empty square for the king to move onto to avoid checkmate.

Exchange Each side swaps pieces.

Exchange, win the One side captures a rook while losing a minor piece. Materially, this favours the player capturing the rook.

Fianchetto The development of a bishop on the long diagonal, e.g. on b2 and g2 for White, or b7 and g7 for Black (see p.135).

Files Straight rows of squares running from one player's side of the board to the other (see p.11).

Flank opening An opening using the a-, b-, c-, f-, g- or h- files (see p.169).

Fork An attack on two pieces by one piece, normally a knight (see p.38).

Gambit An opening where material, usually a pawn, is given up, in the hope of gaining an advantage in development.

Illegal move A move that is not permitted by the laws.

Interpose To place a piece between a piece that is attacked and its attacker.

Isolated pawn A pawn with no pawns of the same colour on the adjoining files (see p.182).

J'adoube A warning by a player that he wishes to adjust a piece without making a move (see p.228).

Kingside The side of the board containing the e-, f-, g- and h-files (see p.10).

Major pieces Queens and rooks (see p.35).

Material The pieces on the board except the king.

Material advantage To have the greatest total value of pieces.

Middlegame The second part of the game, after the opening and before the endgame. There is no clear definition when it begins or ends (see p.172).

Minor Pieces Bishops and knights (see p.35).

Notation The way in which the moves of the game are recorded. Often called the 'score' (see p.12).

Open file A file on which there are no pawns.

Opening The first phase of the game, in which the pieces should be developed (see p.99).

Overloaded piece A piece with too many defensive tasks.

Passed pawn A pawn which does not have an opposing pawn in front of its own file or either adjacent file (see p.184).

Perpetual check A series of checks which cannot be stopped, leading to threefold repetition of position; the game is therefore a draw (see p.220).

Piece

i A chess piece.

ii To 'win a piece' means to capture a bishop or knight.

iii To win a major piece means to capture a queen or rook.

Pin When a piece cannot move without exposing another piece (often the king) to attack (see p.45).

Promotion A pawn, on reaching the farthest rank, may be exchanged for another piece of the same colour, apart from a pawn or king (see p.24).

Queen, to 'To queen a pawn' means to promote a pawn and exchange it for a queen.

Queening square The square on which a pawn is promoted to any other piece of the same colour, apart from a pawn or king (see p.192).

Queenside The side of the board containing the a-, b-, c- and d- files (see p.10).

Ranks Horizontal lines, or rows of squares which run from left to right (see p.11).

Resign To acknowledge defeat, even if not mated.

Sacrifice To give up material in order to achieve a tactical or positional advantage (see p.60).

Skewer A piece is attacked by a less valuable piece. The attacked piece is moved out of the way, so that the attacking piece can capture a piece beyond (see p.49).

Smothered mate A knight mates a king which is surrounded by its own pieces, so that it cannot move (see p.59).

Stalemate A player not in check, who is unable to make a legal move (see p.36).

Under-promotion Promoting a pawn to a rook, knight or bishop (see p.24).

United pawns Pawns of the same colour on adjoining files.

Zugzwang A position in which all legal moves are disadvantageous (see p.210).

8. Laws of chess

These are not all the laws of chess, but the most relevant laws for beginners. For instance, in article 12, on the chess clock, I have only included 2 of the 9 laws. The other 7 deal with arbiters, interruptions, illegal positions, time control, etc., problems which will not take place until one starts playing in club tournaments or congresses.

The official laws of chess and other FIDE (Fédération Internationale des Échecs) regulations, approved by FIDE General Assembly Manila 1992, is printed by B.T. Batsford Limited.

ARTICLE 3: THE RIGHT TO MOVE

3.1 The player with the white pieces commences the game. The players alternate in making one move at a time until the game is completed.

3.2 A player is said to 'have the move' when his opponent's move has been completed (see Article 6).

ARTICLE 4: THE GENERAL DEFINITION OF THE MOVE

4.1 With the exception of castling (see Article 5.1b), a move is the transfer by a player of one of his pieces from one square to another square which is either vacant or occupied by an opponent's piece.

4.2 No piece except the rook when castling (see Article 5.1b) and the knight may cross a square occupied by another piece.

4.3 A piece played to a square occupied by an opponent's piece captures it as part of the same move.

The captured piece must be removed immediately from the chessboard by the player making the capture. (See Article 5.6c for capturing 'en passant'.)

ARTICLE 5: THE MOVES OF THE PIECES

5.1 The King

a Except when castling, the king moves to any adjoining square that is not attacked by an opponent's piece.

b Castling is a move of the king and either rook counting as a single move of the king and executed as follows: the king is transferred from its original square two squares toward either rook on the same rank: then that rook is transferred over the king to the square the king has just crossed.

c If a player touches a rook and then his king he may not castle with that rook and the situation will be governeed by Articles 7.2 and 7.3.

d If a player, intending to castle, touches the king first, or king and rook at the same time, and it then appears that castling is illegal, the player may choose either to move his king or to castle on the other side, provided that castling on that side is legal. If the king has no legal move, the player is free to make any legal move.

e Castling is illegal:
  i If the king has already been moved, or
  ii With a rook that has already been moved.

f Castling is prevented for the time being:
  i If the king's original square or the square which the king must cross over or that which it is to occupy is attacked by an opponent's piece, or
  ii If there is any piece between the king and the rook with which castling is to be effected.

5.6 The Pawn

c A pawn, attacking a square crossed by an opponent's pawn which has been advanced two squares in one move from its original square, may capture this opponent's pawn as though the latter had been moved only one square. This capture may be made only in reply to such an advance and is called an 'en passant' capture.

d On reaching the last rank, a pawn must be immediately exchanged, as part of the same move, for a queen, a rook, a bishop, or a knight of the same colour as the pawn, at the player's choice and without taking into account the other pieces still remaining on the chessboard. This exchange of a pawn for another piece is called 'promotion' and the effect of the promoted piece is immediate.

ARTICLE 6: THE COMPLETION OF THE MOVE

6 A move is completed:

6.1 in the case of the transfer of a piece to a vacant square, when the player's hand has released the piece.

6.2 in the case of a capture, when the captured piece has been removed from the chessboard and the player, having placed his own piece on its new square, has released the piece from his hand;

6.3 in the case of castling, when the player's hand has released the rook on the square crossed by the king. When the player has released the king from his hand, the move is not yet completed, but the player no longer has the right to make any move other than castling on that side, if this is legal.

6.4 in the case of promotion of a pawn, when the pawn has been removed from the chessboard and the player's hand has released the new piece after placing it on the promotion square. If the player has released from his hand the pawn that has reached the promotion square, the move is not yet completed, but the player no longer has the right to play the pawn to another square.

ARTICLE 7: THE TOUCHED PIECE

7.1 Provided that he first expresses his intention (e.g. saying 'J'adoube'), the player having the move may adjust one or more pieces on their squares.

7.2 Except for the above case, if the player having the move deliberately touches on the board:

a One or more pieces of the same colour he must move or capture the first piece touched that can be moved or captured.

b One of his own pieces and one of his opponent's pieces, he must capture his opponent's piece with his own piece or, if this is illegal, move or capture the first piece touched that can be moved or captured. If it is impossible to establish which piece was touched first, the player's piece shall be considered the touched piece.

7.3 If none of the pieces touched has a legal move (or if none of the opponent's pieces touched can be legally captured), the player is free to make any legal move.

7.4 If a player wishes to claim that his opponent has violated Article 7.2, he must do so before he himself touches a piece.

ARTICLE 8: ILLEGAL POSITIONS

8.1 If, during a game, it is found that an illegal move was made, the position shall be reinstated to what it was immediately before the illegal move was made. The game shall then continue by applying the rules of Article 7 to the move replacing the illegal move. If the position cannot be reinstated, the game shall be annulled and a new game played.

This applies to all sessions of play and to a game awaiting a decision by adjudication.

8.2 If, during a game, one or more pieces have been accidentally displaced and incorrectly replaced, the position before the displacement occurred shall be reinstated, and the game shall continue. If the position cannot be reinstated, the game shall be annulled and a new game played.

8.3 If a player moves and in the course of this inadvertently knocks over a piece or several pieces, he must re-establish the position in his own time.

ARTICLE 9: CHECK

9.1 The king is in check when the square it occupies is attacked by one or more of the opponent's pieces; in this case the latter is or are said to be 'checking' the king. A player may not make a move which leaves his king on a square attacked by an opponent's piece.

9.2 Every check must be parried by the move immediately following. If any check cannot be parried, the king is said to be 'checkmated' ('mated'). (See Article 10.1.)

9.3 Declaring a check is not obligatory.

ARTICLE 10: THE COMPLETED GAME

10.1 The game is won by the player who has mated his opponent's king. This immediately ends the game.

10.2 The game is won by the player whose opponent declares he resigns. This immediately ends the game.

10.3 The game is drawn when the king of the player who has the move is not in check and the player cannot make any legal move. The king is then said to be 'stalemated'. This immediately ends the game.

10.4 The game is drawn when one of the following endings arises:

a King against king.

b King against king with only bishop or knight.

c King and bishop against king and bishop, with both bishops on diagonals of the same colour.

This immediately ends the game.

10.5 A player having a bare king cannot win the game. A draw shall be declared if the opponent of a player with a bare king oversteps the time or has sealed an illegal move.

10.6 The game is drawn upon agreement between the players. This immediately ends the game.

10.7 A proposal of a draw under the provisions of Article 10.6 may be made by a player only at the moment when he has just moved a piece.

10.10 The game is drawn, upon a claim by the player having the move, when the same position for the third time:

a Is about to appear if he first writes his move on his score sheet and declares to the arbiter his intention of making this move.

b Has just appeared, the same player having the move each time.

The position is considered the same if pieces of the same kind and colour occupy the same squares and if the possible moves to all the pieces are the same, including the right to castle or to take a pawn en passant.

10.11 If a player executes a move without having claimed a draw for one of the reasons stated in 10.10, he loses the right to claim a draw; this right is restored to him, however, if the same position appears again, the same player having the move.

10.12 The game is drawn when a player having the move claims a draw and demonstrates that at least the last 50 consecutive moves have been made by each side without the capture of any piece and without the movement of any pawn.

ARTICLE 11: THE RECORDING OF GAMES

11.1 In the course of play each player is required to record the game (his own moves and those of his opponent), move after move, as clearly and legibly as possible in the algebraic notation, on the scoresheet prescribed for the competition. It is irrelevant whether the player first makes his move and then records it or vice versa.

11.2 If a player has less than five minutes on his clock until the time control he is not obliged to meet the requirement of Article 11.1. As soon as the special device (e.g. flag) on the clock indicates the end of his allotted time, the player must immediately complete his record of the game by filling in the moves omitted from his scoresheet.

ARTICLE 12: THE CHESS CLOCK

12.1 Each player must make a certain number of moves in an allotted period of time, these two factors being specified in advance. The time saved by a player during one period is added to his time available for the next period.

12.3 At the time determined for the start of the game, the clock of the player who has the white pieces is started. During the game, each of the players, having completed his move, stops his own clock and starts his opponent's clock.

ARTICLE 13: THE ADJOURNMENT OF THE GAME

13.1

a If a game is not finished at the end of the time prescribed for play, the player having the move must write his move in unambiguous notation on his scoresheet, put his scoresheet and that of his opponent in an envelope, seal the envelope, and only then stop his clock without starting his opponent's clock.

b A player having the move who adjourns the game before the end of the playing session will have added to the used time on his clock the whole of the remainnig time to the end of the session.

13.2 Upon the envelope shall be indicated:

a The names of the players.

b The position immediately before the sealed move.

c The time used by each player.

d The name of the player who has sealed the move.

e The number of the sealed move.

13.3 The arbiter is responsible for the safe-keeping of the envelope and should check the accuracy of the information on it.

ARTICLE 14: THE RESUMPTION OF THE ADJOURNED GAME

14.1 When the game is resumed, the position immediately before the sealed move shall be set up on the chessboard, and the time used by each player when the game was adjourned shall be indicated on the clocks.

14.2 The envelope shall be opened only when the player who must reply to the sealed move is present. The player's clock shall be started after the sealed move has been played on the chessboard.

ARTICLE 15: THE CONDUCT OF THE PLAYERS

15.1 Prohibitions

a During play the players are forbidden to make use of handwritten, printed or otherwise recorded matter, or to analyse the game on another chessboard; they are also forbidden to have recourse to the advice or opinion of a third party, whether solicited or not.

b The use of notes made during the game as an aid to memory is also forbidden, aside from the actual recording of the moves and the times on the clocks.

c No analysis is permitted in the playing rooms during play or during resumption sessions.

d It is forbidden to distract or annoy the opponent in any manner whatsoever. This includes the persistent offering of a draw.

ARTICLE 17: SCORING

For a won game the winner gets 1 (one) point and the loser 0 (zero); for a draw each player gets $1/2$ (half) a point.

9. Puzzles

1. How many legal moves does White have at the start of the game?

2. Can White castle: a) kingside? b) queenside?

3. If White plays 1 d8 what pieces can the pawn be promoted to?

4. Black has just played 1...f5. What pawn captures can White make?

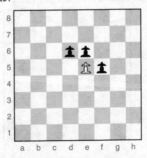

5. Which side is ahead on material?

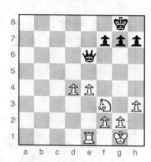

6. How does Black deliver checkmate?

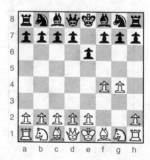

7. How does White deliver checkmate?

8. How does White win?

9. What is this opening called?

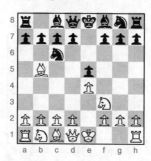

10. How does White force checkmate?

11. How does White force checkmate?

12. How does White 'build a bridge'?

13. Only one move draws for Black. What is it?

14. Can White force the promotion of a pawn?

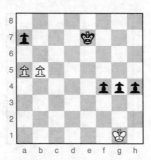

15. How does Black force a draw despite the deficit of two pawns?

16. How does White win? Beware a trap!

17. Can Black escape with a draw, although White has an extra queen?

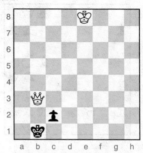

18. How does White win material?

19. How does White force checkmate?

20. How does Black win?

21. How does White win material?

22. How does Black win material?

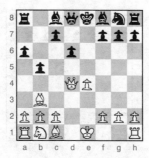

23. How does White win material?

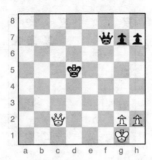

24. How does White win material?

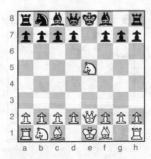

25. How does White force checkmate?

26. How does Black deliver checkmate?

27. How does White force checkmate?

28. How does White force checkmate?

29. How does White win?

30. How does White win?

31. How does Black win?

32. How does Black win material?

10. Solutions to puzzles

1. White has 20 legal moves at the start of the game, 16 with pawns, and four with knights.

2.
- White cannot castle kingside because the bishop on c4 attacks the square f1.
- White can castle queenside. It does not matter that Black's rook on b8 attacks the square b1.

3. White can promote the pawn to a queen, rook, bishop or knight. It does not matter that White already has two knights. In practice White would nearly always promote the pawn to a queen.

4. White can make the captures: 1 exd6 or 1 exf6. It is not possible to capture the black pawn on e6. Remember that pawns capture sideways.

5. Although Black is a queen up, White is ahead on material. White has a rook (5 points), a knight (3 points) and two pawns (2 points), against a queen (9 points). So White is (5+3+2) 10 against 9 ahead.

6. The move Qh4 is checkmate, an example of fool's mate. This rarely happens in practice.

7. The move Qxf7 is checkmate. Beware! This often occurs.

8. 1 Nxe5 Bxd1 2 Bxf7+ Ke7 3 Nd5 mate.

9. Ruy Lopez or Spanish Opening.

10. The quickest way to force checkmate is: 1 Qg7 Kd8 2 Qd7 mate. 1 Qf6 would be a blunder because Black would be in stalemate.

11. The black king escapes, for the time being, after 1 Kc2 Ka3. So White should instead play a waiting move, such as 1 Rb7. White then checkmates after 1...Ka3 2 Ra7 mate or, after 1 Rb7, 1...Ka1 2 Kc2 Ka2 3 Ra8 mate.

12. 1 Re4 leads to the Lucena position.

13. The only move to draw is 1...Ke8, e.g. 2 Kd6 Kd8 3 e7+ Ke8 4 Ke6 stalemate.

14. White forces the promotion of a pawn by 1 b6 axb6 2 a6! and Black's king is outside the square. Not 2 axb6? Kd6 and Black's king is inside the square. Also possible is 1 a6 Kd7 2 b6 Kc8 3 bxa7 and queens.

15. After 1...Rd1+ 2 Rf1 Rxf1+ 3 Kxf1 Bh3! 4 gxh3 (otherwise Black plays 4...Bxg2) White is left with h-pawns with the wrong colour queening square for the bishop and so the position is drawn.

16. White wins most quickly by the underpromotion 1 f8/R! Kh6 2 Rh8 mate. Not 1 f8/Q stalemate.

17. Black can draw by 1...Ka1! when 2 Qxc2 is stalemate. Not 1...Kc1 when White wins by bringing up the king.

18. White wins Black's queen by the fork 1 Ne7+.

19. White can force a smothered mate by 1 Qc4+ Kh8 2 Nf7+ Kg8 (after 2...Rxf7 3 Qb8+ leads to a back rank mate) 3 Nh6+! Kh8 4 Qg8+! Rxg8 5 Nf7 mate.

20. Black wins by 1...Qb2! and now:
- 2 Qxb2 Rd1 with a back rank mate.
- 2 Qe1 Qxc3! 3 Qxc3 Rd1+ mating.
- 2 Rc2 Qb1+ 3 Qf1 Qxc2 winning a rook, more than enough to guarantee a win.

21. White wins the exchange by the fork 1 Nf6+. Black cannot reply 1...gxf6 because the pawn is pinned.

22. Black traps White's bishop on b3 by 1...c5!, e.g. 2 Qd5 Be6 (not 2...c4? 3 Qxa8) 3 Qc6+ Bd7 4 Qd5 c4.

23. White wins Black's queen by the skewer 1 Qa2+.

24. White wins Black's queen by the discovered check 1 Nc6+.

The remaining puzzles are all taken from real games between famous players.

25. White forces checkmate by the queen sacrifice 1 Qxf8+! Kxf8 2 Bh6+ Kg8 3 Re8 – a variety of back rank mate.
(Judit Polgar – then aged 12 – v Angelova, Thessaloniki 1988.)

26. 1...Bb4! is checkmate because White is in double check from the bishop on b4 and the queen on e8. White can get out of either check but not both.
(Lehmann v Teschner, Bad Pyrmont 1950.)

27. White forces checkmate by 1 Qb8+! (decoying Black's knight) 1...Nxb8 2 Rd8 mate.
(Morphy v The Duke of Brunswick and Count Isouard in consultation, Paris 1858.)

28. White forces checkmate by the queen sacrifice
1 Qd8+ Kxd8 2 Bg5 double check and now:
- 2...Ke8 3 Rd8 mate.
- 2...Kc7 3 Bd8 mate.

(**Reti v Tartakower, Vienna 1910**.)

29. White wins by 1 Be8! exploiting the weakness of
Black's back rank, e.g.
- 1...Rxe8 2 Qxf8+ Rxf8 3 Rxf8 mate.
- 1...Be7 2 Qf8+ Bxf8 3 Rxf8 mate.

30. White won by 1 Qh8+ (deflecting Black's king and
even stronger than 1 Nxf7) 1...Kxh8 2 Nxf7+ (forking
Black's king and queen) 2...Kg7 3 Nxg5 and White
emerged a knight and pawn up with an easy win in
view. Black resigned.

(**Petrosian v Spassky, World Championship 1966**.)

31. Black traps White's queen by 1...Ne3! If
2 fxe3 Qh4+ 3 g3 Qxg3 mate.

(**Normally quoted as Gibaud v Lazard, Paris 1924,
but some chess historians claim the game is a hoax**.)

32. Black could have won a pawn by 1...Bxa3!, e.g.
- 2 Rxa3 Qxc1+.
- 2 bxa3 Qc3+ and 3...Qxa1.
In fact both world champions overlooked this
possibility and the game finally ended in a draw after
1...a4.

(**Kasparov v Karpov, Linares 1994**.)

COLLINS

Other Gem titles that may interest you include:

Gem Party Games
A varied collection of over 200 games suitable for all age groups to play at parties **£3.50**

Gem Travel Games
An indispensable help in keeping children amused on journeys **£3.50**

Gem Holiday Games
A handy-sized guide to a wide range of indoor and outdoor games to play on holiday **£3.50**

Gem Card Games
A compact guide to the rules and strategies of play for a wide range of popular family card games **£3.50**

Gem Games for One
Features over 100 games and activities to play by yourself **£3.50**

Gem Children's Games
Children's ball games, singing games and word games for every occasion **£3.50**

COLLINS

Bestselling Collins Gem titles include:

Gem English Dictionary (£3.50)
Gem Calorie Counter (£2.99)
Gem Thesaurus (£2.99)
Gem French Dictionary (£3.50)
Gem German Dictionary (£3.50)
Gem Basic Facts Mathematics (£2.99)
Gem Birds Photoguide (£3.50)
Gem Wild Flowers Photoguide (£3.50)
Gem Card Games (£3.50)
Gem World Atlas (£3.50)